Inside the Music

INSIDE THE MUSIC

Conversations with Contemporary
Musicians about Spirituality, Creativity,
and Consciousness

Dimitri Ehrlich

Shambhala   Boston & London   1997

This book is dedicated to Gregory Hayden Brown (1966-1990),
who showed me a lot of things about music and life and death,
to Ron Wilbur (1965-1997), whose intelligence, humor, and "thereness"
were bedrock, and to Max Hayden Menken, age two, who is
teaching me to dance.

Shambhala Publications, Inc.
Horticultural Hall
300 Massachusetts Avenue
Boston, MA 02115
http://www.shambhala.com

Some portions of the chapter on Mick Jagger have
appeared previously in slightly different form in the
New York Times (December 24, 1995) and in *Interview*
magazine (October 1994). Some portions of the chapter
on Jeff Buckley have appeared previously in slightly
different form in the *London Observer* (January 8, 1995).

9 8 7 6 5 4 3 2 1

First Edition
Printed in the United States of America
⊗ This edition is printed on acid-free paper that meets the
American National Standards Institute Z39.48 Standard.
Distributed in the United States by Random House, Inc.,
and in Canada by Random House of Canada Ltd

Library of Congress Cataloging-in-Publication Data

Ehrlich, Dimitri.
  Inside the music: conversations with contemporary musicians
about spirituality, creativity, and consciousness / Dimitri Ehrlich.—
1st Shambhala ed.
    p. cm.
  ISBN 1-57062-273-6 (pbk.: alk. paper)
  1. Musicians—20th century—Interviews. 2. Music—20th
century—Philosophy and aesthetics. I. Title.
ML385.E37 1997   97-20986
781'.1—dc21   CIP
                                                       MN

CONTENTS

ACKNOWLEDGMENTS

If it weren't for my mother and father, Dr. Milton Paul Ehrlich and Dr. Etta B. Ehrlich, who exposed my brother and sister and me to meditation, yoga, and tai chi when we were very small children, this book would not exist. Thanks to my parents also for the music with which they raised me, especially the Rolling Stones and the Krishna chants and the Jewish folk songs, and for saying mantras together. Most important, thanks to my parents for their love and friendship, both spiritual and regular style. Special gratitude to my brother, Gregor, for tolerating and living with me, to Alexis and Bruce for their encouragement, and also to Leah Santoro, for putting up with me during the time that I wrote this. Sam Dock, who helped research, arrange, and transcribe artist interviews, was a source of considerable emotional and practical support. Gregor, Stephen Greco, Clare Bundy, and Jon Moskowitz all get gold merit stars for reading and criticizing early drafts. Special respect to the lama Gelek Rinpoche and the Jewel Heart for education. Maximum gratitude to Andrew Blauner, secret agent, for suggesting that I write this book, to editor Peter Turner for making me feel it was possible, and to *Shambhala Sun* editor Melvin McLeod for making the writing better. Also, there were twenty musicians who gave their time and thoughtfulness, and for that the words *thank you* seem too small. May readers enjoy and take inspiration from the words of these musicians, and may any benefit that I have gained from writing this book be shared with all sentient beings pervading space.

Regarding the Photographs: Special appreciation goes to Anna Gabriel, who roamed with an open heart and open eyes to photograph many of the artists included here.

I would also like to thank C. B. Smith for the photo of Perry Farrell; Jesse Frohman for the beautiful image of Meredith Monk; and Bruce Weber for the portrait of Jeff Buckley. (In addition to being a magnificent photographer, Bruce is an active supporter of Green Chimneys, an agency that makes rehabilitation of injured wildlife part of its treatment program for emotionally and physically handicapped juveniles. Green Chimneys is located at P.O. Box 719, Putnam Lake Road, Brewster, NY 10509-0719.)

INTRODUCTION

About ten years ago, while writing and recording some songs, I began to wonder about the impact that meditation could have on the process of creating music. My mother had given me my first instruction in meditation—what she called sensory awareness—when I was about ten years old, while she and my father were doing research for an article on meditating with the whole family (think Brady Bunch, mid-seventies hippies style). But it wasn't until a decade later that I began to practice meditation in earnest and to experience the subtle shifts in consciousness that can accompany any other consistent, formal practice of mindfulness.

It wasn't anything earthshaking. It wasn't even about doing anything. It was the realization that just being attentive to what goes on in your mind, the very fact of awareness, changes what goes on in your mind. That's all. It's Heisenberg's uncertainty principle applied to consciousness: things observed behave differently than things unobserved.

I realized that awareness could make a difference in the process of making music and wondered if the listener could actually hear that difference. After all, if the mind of the musician is functioning with more awareness, wouldn't his or her music be better in some way?

There are two schools of thought on this. John Cleese once said that being neurotic—and hence at the mercy of unconscious patterns and reactions—was great for his art. Once he went into therapy, a large part of his drive to make comedy was gone. And as sybarite and writer William S. Burroughs noted while on a two-week meditation retreat with the Tibetan lama Chögyam Trungpa in 1976, maybe the goals of self-realization and art are not compatible:

> I use meditation to get material for writing. I am not concerned with some abstract nirvana. It is exactly the visions and fireworks that are useful to me, exactly what all the masters tell us we should pay as little attention to as possible. Telepathy, journey out of the body—these manifestations, according to Trungpa, are mere distractions. Exactly. Distractions: fun, like hang-gliding or surfboarding or skin diving. So why not have fun? I sense an underlying sense of dogma here to which I am not willing to submit. The purpose of the bodhisattva and an artist are different and perhaps not reconcilable. Show me a good Buddhist novelist.

Burroughs's point was that it's better to be a little nutty and to lack self-knowledge if you want to be a great artist. After all, Jimi Hendrix wasn't exactly a paragon of mental stability, and great artists from van Gogh to Kurt Cobain have exhibited a serious lack of impulse control. Maybe badly socialized musicians are endowed with some kind of wisdom of which their art is a manifestation, some inherent awareness that provides a sensitivity to deeper realms of experience.

On the other hand, contrary to what John Cleese and William Burroughs suggest, perhaps the process of developing insight into yourself can make you a better musician. Maybe sanity is good for art. As the singer-songwriter Mark Everett, frontman for the Eels, told the *Los Angeles Times*, "A lot of artists fear therapy because they think they're gonna get happy and they're not gonna have anything to write about anymore. It's done the opposite for me. 'Cause I realize I'm not just gonna get happy, I'm just gonna become more aware and learn how to deal with things a little better." When interviewed for this book, Philip Glass pointed out that people have romanticized the idea of the artist as nut-job and associate wild behavior with artistic greatness, when in fact no such link necessarily exists. And Allen Ginsberg articulated the idea that creativity and meditation could be inextricably linked, under the general heading "first thought/best thought." Basically, that means that if you watch what comes up in the mind-stream with precision, vivid images will present themselves effortlessly and creating will become more like transcription.

In writing this book I spoke with a wide cross section of musicians to look at the role that spirituality, religion, and personal philosophy play in the making of contemporary music. As always, there are musicians who find religion too entrapping, too reminiscent of what they've been running away from all their lives. But many others want to find out more about spirituality, whether within a particular tradition or not.

What is spirituality? After speaking with the musicians featured in this book, I came to think about spirituality in a new way: an understanding that the material world is not the end of the story, that things are impermanent, almost dreamlike. It's what I call a ventilating worldview, in which phenomenal reality seems less solid, somehow more airy and permeable. Spirituality, for many of the people I spoke to, certainly does not require anything like a firm deistic belief system. That's one of the good things about contemporary music and pop culture: its openness and inclusivity. Spirituality among contemporary musicians includes everything from traditional Christianity to just deeply wanting to know the meaning of life—what Buddhists call the Great Doubt. Reading this book will be frustrating unless you accept the fact that nobody here knows definitively what he or she is talking about. Jeff Buckley said it best: "The only thing I'm sure of is that I don't know anything for sure, so it would probably be best to track me down in a few years and talk with me some more then." (Buckley, who I believe was among the most original musical voices of the last decade, was thirty years old when he died in a drowning accident a few months after I interviewed him for this book.)

One question I've wondered about for years is whether spiritual change in a musician's mind affects the music that he or she makes—can you hear the effects of variations in consciousness in their music? After having written this book, I now feel the answer to that is yes but it's a vague yes because the influence of spirituality on popular music has been so complex that it's impossible to reach any simple conclusion about its impact.

Rock and religion have been intertwined for years. In the 1960s, the Beatles became entranced by an Indian Hindu guru named Maharishi Mahesh Yogi; as a result, George Harrison introduced sitar into Beatles recordings, and pop lyrics took on a mystical bent. In the 1970s, Cat Stevens became a Muslim; as a result, he retired from his professional life as a musician and donated most of his money to an Islamic school. In the 1980s Bob Dylan explored his Jewish heritage and for a while was a born-again Christian; the recordings he made reflected his newfound faith. Of course, gospel played a crucial role in the historic development of rock and roll, and today contemporary Christian music is among the fastest-growing genres.

The fact that some rock stars, members of a profession notorious for its egocentricity, are developing an interest in Eastern philosophies such as Buddhism, which teach the emptiness of ego, is not without irony. But the Tibetan lama Gelek Rinpoche thinks that music has a clear spiritual purpose and musicians are well suited to spiritual practice. "I've talked to a couple of musicians. They're very nice people and I don't think their values are so bad," says Gelek Rinpoche. "I think that their aim is to please people. Somebody, I think it was Allen Ginsberg, asked me a question: 'What is the purpose of music, in your opinion?' I said, 'To eliminate suffering and give people relief and an opportunity to rest and take a break.' And that's what many musicians do. Whenever I talk to entertainers, my view is that they're totally focused on the best way they can sing so that people will enjoy it. All this entertainment has its purpose: to eliminate suffering of people. Why do you think people turn to the rock stars? Because they give them some sense of relief. People are tired of always working, being under pressure, tired of life itself, so it's a little relief they're getting. I think it's a great service, I look at it that way."

Shortly before his death, Jimi Hendrix began to speak of the healing power of music. That music has spiritual power is a given. Popular music is one of the great conveyors of consciousness of our time. We don't look at music as a source of education, but it is. If a singer is drawing your attention to the shape of a woman's ass, that's education—that is what you are training your mind to think is important. Entertainment is always teaching us something. When the radio is playing in the supermarket, you are meditating on romantic love. If you listen to hip-hop every day, you are meditating on Glocks, blunts, and hos. You are visualizing drive-by shootings, and Snoop is your guru. There is no such thing as "just entertainment."

If you are absorbing information—whether it's in the lyrics or the vibe of the music—you are training your mind in a particular direction.

This book has been custom-made to fit the twin obsessions of my life: music and spirituality. Although I'm not a Christian, I've long been addicted to the power of gospel music, and love being around it. But The Rolling Stones are the band that most directly affected my life. I used to joke that they actually reorganized my DNA: When I was at college, my bed was made of a plywood plank resting on cinder blocks. I used to lie there and listen to *Exile on Mainstreet* and *Some Girls* and *Tattoo You* and *Black and Blue*—meditate on them, really. I would feel the music vibrate my bed, gently sending those echoes of thought made manifest in music right into my spine. I felt something change in me as a result of not only hearing the music but feeling it.

Years later, when I met Keith Richards and told him that his music had changed my life, he raised his plastic jug of beer and, cracking a leathery crocodile smile, said, "As long as it's for the better, darling, as long as it's for the better."

The fact that music can change you, for better or worse, is one of the fundamental premises of this book. Of course, it's not what kind of music you listen to that matters, but how you listen to it. Sacredness is something the listener imputes. There are roles that music can play in your life, ways of relating to it that feel not only pleasurable but cosmically right. If that kind of active listening is somehow good for you than, yes, Keith, the music has probably changed us for the better—even if it's only rock-and-roll.

PERRY FARRELL

PERRY FARRELL

The Art of Staying Cheerful When the Sound System Goes Down

I have to admit, although it is one of the most shameful things for a music journalist to confess, especially one in the employ of a magazine (*Interview*) that prides itself on being cutting-edge, that I fully missed the boat on Perry Farrell. Missed the boat so completely that the boat had not only departed but arrived at the other shore—the waves had stopped, the boat was tied up at the dock, and the passengers had all disembarked before I caught on to *Nothing's Shocking*, the 1988 major label debut album by Farrell in his first incarnation as leader of the quixotic art-rock band Jane's Addiction. That album reintroduced art rock as a popular musical form and raised the level of discourse in pop music. With his next band, Porno For Pyros, Farrell proved it was possible to be simultaneously conceptual and unpretentious and still have stainless indie cred. All of which sailed right over my head, until I went to Woodstock.

Although he is perhaps best known for conceiving and organizing the most successful touring rock festival of modern times, Lollapalooza, I didn't see Perry Farrell perform until Porno For Pyros played at Woodstock '94, the most shamelessly retrogressive rock concert of modern times. I was in a bad mood, but Farrell proved that even the most corporately sponsored reenactments of peace, love, and good vibrations need not be cause for despair. I had driven up to Saugerties, New York, and decamped among the mud people and naked frat boys, expecting mostly drizzle and nostalgia. Hunkered down in the shit mist with a bad attitude, I was totally unprepared for the freshness of Farrell's performance. It stood out amid all that yearning for the past like a warm, clean piece of bright green Astroturf floating in the mud.

You haven't really experienced true mud until you've slogged through a field where half a million white people have just spent forty-eight hours throwing the ultimate frat party in the pouring rain. The mud was mixed with sweat, urine, and beer and tromped into ghoulish oatmeal. Kids were running and diving head-first into it, line after line of young men who looked strangely like marines, leaping face forward into the earth. It was very unhygienic. One kid had a bloody lip, another had a gash on the bridge of his nose, but there was no concern for germs. A girl with no shirt was being photographed squeezing her muddy breasts together. A young hairdresser from Long Island stabbed a can of beer with a pen knife so that she could drink it from the small puncture she'd made in the side. "It's called a shotgun. It gets ya drunk faster. I wanna get wasted."

All of this unseemliness was presaged by rumors that had begun to circulate two days earlier. Apparently security personnel had unearthed several hundred vials of crack and an Uzi that some forward-looking soul had buried beneath the lawn of the concert site. There were to be a thousand security officers, metal detectors, lots of storm fencing and guard dogs, and an absolute ban on alcohol, drugs, weapons, or sharpened objects of any kind. Even tent pegs were forbidden.

For a festival ostensibly dedicated to progressive

thinking, Woodstock was not a pleasant place for vegetarians. The smell of fecal bolus wafted up from the overtaxed Porta-San village, where two-ton trucks—literally shit-suckers—were vacuuming doody out of the latrines. Neither I nor my companion, a Quaker with an impacted colon, had excreted for forty-eight hours.

The mud took on its own visceral beauty, like luscious chocolate icing that some benevolent baker had spread all over the surface of the earth. It was everywhere, so there was no point in fighting it. I was going to slosh through the crud to test some of the Woodstock pizza, but the shit stink was burning my eyes. The mud people were forming congo lines and sashaying through the sea of bodies. The collective grumpiness factor was reaching a threshold point. (Psychedelics and alcohol can only go so far to ameliorate conditions of prolonged physical unpleasantness, particularly when the misery is not only self-inflicted but in many cases costs $135 a ticket.) The odor was so severe that although I am allergic to cigarette smoke, I was begging my Quaker friend to smoke a cigarette and blow the smoke in my face. Cancer before shit death.

A disturbingly steady flow of bodies were being carried out on stretchers. Afterward, one of the directors of medical services said he would have preferred to have been in the Vietnamese or Korean War for those forty-eight hours.

At last Perry Farrell, a man who knows a thing or two about promoting concerts, came onstage with Porno For Pyros. Unlike most of the acts before his, who were either genuine ex-hippies or struggling wanna-be hippies, Farrell and his group dressed in slick lamé suits and ties, swathed in an irony that was perfectly up-to-date. But he didn't just look like he was free from the deadly nostalgia of the event—he talked and rocked that way too. In one between-song comment about guns in high schools, Farrell said, "I liked how it used to be. You didn't like a man, you punched him in the face." That was about the extent of his hippie nostalgia.

Porno For Pyros staged an avant-garde theatrical performance replete with mimes and dancers, accompanied by their high-concept psycho-pop, all original and perfectly contemporary. In fact, almost all of the material was brand-new. "I know it's Woodstock, but we're trying out some new songs," Farrell shouted at one point. "What if I die tomorrow? You want me to play yesterday's song? Fuck off!"

Porno For Pyros dished up primal noise while Farrell bleated out a disjointed harmonica line and two female strippers simulated lesbian sex and undressed to their G-strings and pasties. Farrell dove into the audience and was passed around. The music evinced the fragmentation and overload of the generation he was playing to more successfully than any of the bands before or after.

"Chaos is a beautiful thing!" Farrell said, acknowledging his mastery of it as he spun a lingerie-clad gymnast who had climbed a rope far above the stage. A scary clown covered in tattoos minced around Farrell and drew a bloody dollar sign on his own body with red lipstick. Farrell's act was riveting and totally surefooted: he sang into the crotch of a topless fire-eater as she twirled flaming batons.

There is something hallucinatory about Perry Farrell's singing, something disconcerting, like the ground shifting slightly beneath your feet. The air of controlled tension is so strong in his recent music that he hardly ever needs to unleash the squall of layered guitars that typified Jane's Addiction, and there's a sense of impending explosion that lends force to his high, dreamy voice. He's like a satyr you might dream was approaching you if you had huffed too many industrial solvents. In fact, everything about Farrell's voice suggests that you have been sniffing glue, though not on purpose—because that would at least put you in the driver's seat. The unsettling thing is that you're not sure if you're experiencing an auditory hallucination or if that weird, filtered, melting sound is objectively in his voice. It's as though every time you listen to him sing, you unconsciously have the sneaking suspicion that a tasteless, colorless, psychoactive mist may be seeping out of your radiator.

But the feeling he gives you, that someone might have slipped you a mickey, doesn't fully explain Farrell's achievement. For that we need to get historical for a moment. In the late 1980s, everything shocking had been done, and then undone by punk, and then re-done by the new wave. And then, when the era of the Big Hair Bands had descended on the wings of MTV and made believe it was all new again, Farrell recorded *Nothing's Shocking* and made rock that actually seemed new. More than that, he made rock itself seem new again, not because he reinvented everything but because he questioned it.

A lot of the beauty in Farrell's work isn't melodic or rhythmic, it's just the fact that you feel like he's not relying on clichés. There's an ominous excitement in hearing a man operate without a safety net. Perry Farrell is so fully himself that we feel we are somehow accompanying him on some brave charge into the future. He accomplishes that by throwing away ideas as fast as he can. He has a confidence in the rightness of being himself that's as complete as anything since Dylan reinvented the look, sound, and meaning of rock all at once. Although Farrell's talent and ambition are not so great as Dylan's, his vision is sufficiently singular and acidic to cut through the pretense and sameness of "alternative rock," whose armies of same-sounding drones were already threatening to strip the word *alternative* of any meaning by the time Farrell performed at Woodstock.

Outwardly Farrell appears willing to work within the conventions of rock, but he subverts those conventions, corroding and recontextualing them. Hokier than the hokiest of snake oil salesmen, Farrell is able to dive head-long into the old-school theatrics of the pre-rock and roll era and salvage from it so much of what alternative rock's irony police have rejected. Hence, when Lollapalooza first went on the road, it had elements of a seedy, small-time carnival, including the Jim Rose Side Show, a freak act in which a man punctured himself with needles. This wasn't repackaged rock theater from the Fillmore—it was more like Barnum and Bailey: low-down, old-school, fat lady, strong man, freak show theatrics.

As the founder of Lollapalooza, Farrell gave a generation its own traveling version of Woodstock, an alternative rock tour de force, which became so big, so powerful, and so popular that Farrell had to jump off. He eventually disassembled his band, Jane's Addiction, and formed Porno For Pyros for the same reason: Jane's Addiction was becoming so successful that he felt the band's next artistic move was being stifled by people's expectations. Today, with a slightly lower profile and a mind focused on reinvention, Farrell is playing to smaller crowds but he's adamant about creating art on his own terms. Operating with that sense of freedom, he's been finding not only artistic rejuvenation but a kind of spiritual one as well.

"Whether it's about being a catalyst or being another cell in the total living organism, I'm finding that in the nineties, this is what I'm shooting for, this is what I believe: I believe that the next step for entertainers is to teach people self-love.

"Those who separate themselves, those who look down, those who condescend, they are going to be wiped out. I think that people are just going to wipe them off the slate. The performers who will be valued are those who come to a town and practice and exhibit self-love. Because I think that what we want now is to learn how to love ourselves, or—why don't I just put it on me?—I have to learn how to love myself."

How can music help people work toward such a lofty goal? Farrell's solution sounds Taoist: know who you are, and be who you are. By Farrell settling fully into the pleasure of his work, there will be a trickle-down effect on his audience, so concerts become something he experiences with them rather than something he does for them. Don't just sing songs that tell people, Don't worry, be happy; manifest that advice and exude it.

"What I'm trying to do in my life right now is learn how to love the position I'm in. I welcome the fact that I entertain people. I don't separate myself from them, I don't look down at the crowd. I like being the emcee at the party, I like putting people in a good mood, and I work hard to do it.

"If I can show you that I love what I'm doing, that I love my situation, then you're gonna see my confidence and say, 'What is it that makes this man so centered that he can love what he's doing? Because that's what I pick up from him now.' "

Farrell believes that the relationship between performer and audience can sometimes involve a subtle power play, wherein the artist's ego is built up at the expense of the fans' self-esteem. And while he admits that in the past he may have been guilty of performing within that paradigm, he's recently begun reassessing the way fame has affected him. Having experienced enough of the rock and roll fantasy to know that it is, after all, a fantasy, he has begun to search for something more gratifying than the one dimensional rock-star lifestyle. One can't really know that materialistic success is ultimately unsatisfactory until one has tasted a certain amount of it, and in that sense Farrell's attitude is a luxury. It reflects the thinking of a person who's experienced a certain amount of financial reward and begun to look for philosophical satisfaction by reexamining his relationship to his audiences.

"As you get older, you try to think things out. As I started to have success, I started to wonder what I was going to do with it. This is kind of funny, but a big milestone was O. J. Simpson's case. I saw that he took his success and used it to abuse other people and himself. I mean, 'giving back to the community' is kind of a cliché, but how about 'redistributing your luck'? That's a nicer term. Or maybe refine it a little bit more: 'redistribution of luck.' One man can't take all the success and keep it for himself. So I started wondering, how am I gonna make it through this world? I see a lot of people who get fame in the music industry, and for the most part, it's fleeting. I started to wonder, well, what about karmic law? What if you gave it back? And I practiced it, and it worked. You know, I spent all the money I made from the Lollapalooza festival, and more, all my savings, to do this Enid Festival, which is a multimedia and music tour. And I found that something very big happened to me, something much bigger than if I had just spent my good fortune from Lollapalooza on myself. I mean that inside of me, I got a feeling of a giant. Lollapalooza was a great thing to me, but it is the way of man to diminish the full and replenish the humble. So all of a sudden here comes the backlash and how do you get past it? You have to be humble and give away the fortune that you got, and then you get blessed again. There's a system to it.

"When I was performing, I used to wonder if people liked me and I tried very hard to please them. I had this feeling that I wasn't fully whole and the audience was gonna tell me whether I'm good or not with their applause. Now my attitude is that the people wouldn't be there if they didn't enjoy it. So I have to go up there loving what I'm gonna do, not dreading it. I have to look at the audience with open eyes and give 'em everything in my body.

"By the end of the show, I've sweated as much as a man could sweat in an hour and a quarter and I'm fully exhausted. But I have to tell you that my healthiest times in life are either when I'm on a full vacation, when I'm surfing, or when I'm fully working, when I'm on the road. I get superstrong, both physically and mentally."

Among Farrell's great strengths as a performer is his capacity to retain what Zen practitioners call a beginner's mind. He seems to approach music as a form of self-education, what the Buddhist scholar Robert Thurman termed evolutionary sport, meaning his attitude is as playful as it is focused on creative self-realization. "There are so many things I'm still learning. Believe me, I am by no means a master yet at what I want to accomplish, which is making the party happen. I'm so interested in what makes people enjoy themselves and how to bring joy to them. Let me tell you a few of the things I've learned just on my recent tour. I used to get angry when the sound was bad. Then I realized two things. Number one, I believe in the spirit world, and I believe the spirit works through a lot of things, one of them being electricity. The spirit works in mischievous, roundabout ways, and if it wants to give you

strength of character, it tests you by offering you a di-
lemma such as 'Hey, the sound doesn't work right.' So how
do you react? Do you get angry or do you laugh it off and
look at the crowd and show them that it doesn't throw you?
Because things being spontaneous and live, seven out of
ten times, it's going to happen, and you can't expect perfection. Now, when you get mad, it only puts the crowd in
a bad mood, too. It's like you're a paternal figure, and
when the father is upset, the little child gets upset too,
without even knowing why. That's what would happen
when I would play in a bad mood. So it's up to me: can I
stay in a good mood in the midst of malfunction?

"If you can stay loose and humorous, the show ends
up being loose and humorous. Two shows ago, I had a
splitting headache; I was in the worst mood, hadn't been
to bed, and the bass from the opening band was just thud-
ding up my neck into my brain, and the backstage was just
a bathroom. But I got out there and I turned the thing
around by getting light. Getting light and being in a good
mood. It also helps to have nice wine. I mean, there are
tricks.

"If your intention is, 'I want to enlighten these people, give light to these people,' then you know you're not
helping things by losing your cool, even when things aren't
working."

From a theatrical point of view, the greater the level
of artifice, the greater the level of risk. If you're going to
walk onstage in the same ripped jeans you've lived in for
the last week and play seventy-two-bar guitar solos with
your back to the audience in the mode of the Allman
Brothers, you can't really fall very far, because from a theatrical standpoint, you're not exposing yourself to much
risk. If, on the other hand, you're going to create a complex and highly staged performance with acrobats and

flamethrowers—as Farrell did when he played at Wood-stock—the risk is enormous.

Another drawback of the more overtly theatrical side of rock performance is that, although the potential for entertainment value may be higher, the artist is also setting up more of a barrier between the band and the audience. "Agreed, agreed. You don't want barriers. I'll tell you what I do these days. What I want to do is dissolve the boundaries. I want to become them. There's real beauty in what's going on now with the rave scene because the event is the people. I love that idea: the event is the people, the people are the event. So how do I do that when I'm performing? Of course I don't like to just steal people's ideas, but my artistry has always included garbage picking, garbage collecting. I pick little things off of people, I get inspiration off of 'em, and then I put it into a mix. It's like being a good cook: there's not an ingredient that anyone ever invented, but a good cook is someone who knows how to take things and make them taste good together, collectively."

By communicating with his fans through the Internet, Farrell has been able to prearrange for certain audience members to join him onstage during each show of his most recent tour. He has also redesigned his stage to create a kind of theater-in-the-round environment, which downplays the separation between performer and audience. "What I like to do these days is to keep the room circular; I put risers behind the drummer and on the side of the stage. And I use the computer to get people in each city we play in, to dance and to sing. So when we come into a town we've already been in communication with people via the Internet, and I have dancers and singers that I've never met before. What this does is change the focal point: rather than its being just me on a stage, the dancers are behind us, and the crowd is dancing in front of us, and the shows have been a lot looser. I'm surrounded by people, and we're centrifugal, and it's making the room spin. It's the same thing with the lights: the lights are no longer focused straight at the band, they revolve around the room."

By inviting increasing amounts of audience interaction, Farrell has introduced an element of uncertainty, because no matter how tight his band is, the fans he connects with on the Internet have only had one rehearsal. "When we get there, they come downstairs, and while we get dressed, we rehearse. So we have a little run-through, and my attitude is, and I might be cutting my own throat here, but I think that anybody can sing. It just makes everybody feel like, the show is us. I have a few people who know the words sing into the mike, and if some of them really can't sing, at least the people who are singing closer to the mike can. The audience sings too, and this is one of the most beautiful things about our show. Like I say, everything's always evolving as to how the evening goes, how the show should evolve, what's working and what's not, and is it making people happier? And what I'm finding is that people love to sing. The audience sings really loud. So now I'm building songs that work with the digital world, the organic musician world, and that always includes the folk end of the spectrum, which is the sing-along. What I love these days about writing songs is that I always plan a spot where there's a sing-along, because there's nothing more beautiful. If you've ever gone to Mexico, you know they have these classic songs and they sing 'em at restaurants— there's something very ancient and bonding about the chorus, the sing-along. These are songs that represent one's country or one's race. For me it's the human race. 'Happy Birthday' is like that. Even though people sing out of tune, when the whole world sings, it's right on key."

In keeping with Farrell's emphasis on the group sing-along as a key element in his performances, he is increasingly interested in applying the same principle to songwriting, in an approach reminiscent of the paranormal phenomenon sometimes referred to as automatic writing. This means writing with as little active consciousness of the self as possible. This involves decreasing the individual's sense of authorship or ownership of the creative process and conceiving of music as the property of the collective unconscious, which the artist taps into, serving as a conduit rather than creator per se. "I might have written a particular song, but it might have been automatic writing done on behalf of all of us. That's what I kinda hope when I write a song. I mean, the best songs take no effort. There's nothing you can say that hasn't been said; as I said, you can only take ingredients that already exist. You can't invent music; I don't think it's possible. You can only admire."

PHILIP GLASS

A Question of Motivation

When I was eleven years old and my brother was nine, a well-intentioned family friend drove us into Brooklyn one night to see *Satyagraha*, the avant-garde opera by Philip Glass. He gave us the tickets, dropped us off at the Brooklyn Academy of Music, and said, "Have a good time." We had no idea what we were in for. Setting aside that we were too young to sit through a traditional opera, much less a difficult, pioneering work that combined pulsing minimalist motifs with a text based on the Bhagavad Gita and sung in Sanskrit; setting aside that my eleven-year-old's attention span did not allow me to appreciate melodies consisting of the tones from E to E on the white notes of a piano repeated thirty-six times; and setting aside that I had barely any idea who the opera's protagonist, Gandhi, was, it was a totally worthwhile experience. Worthwhile mainly because, years later when I met Philip Glass at a dinner party, I was able to mention casually that I'd seen his groundbreaking opera as an eleven-year-old. I may have had to sit through several hours of what was then indecipherable sonic torture, but payback came in the form of some excellent cocktail chat.

I suppose Glass has had his payback, too. After years of anonymous and commercially difficult struggle as a member of the downtown New York avant-garde, Glass has become that most unusual of artistic specimens: a living classical composer who is also a household name. *Time* magazine has called him "today's most innovative composer," and *Rolling Stone* said he was "the best-known living classical composer on the planet."

Glass is a sleepy-eyed man who tends toward well-worn corduroys, rumpled sweaters, and a perpetually distracted air. But he didn't make it to the apex of modern American music by shuffling along in a pair of flip-flops. Highly educated and extremely articulate, he is a shrewd player in the art mafia world of modern experimental music, where grant money and critical notice are the subjects of fierce competition.

He is also a hard worker. When I called him at his "retreat" home in Nova Scotia, he said that one of the reasons he has for so long been able to work for eleven or twelve hours a day is because of the meditative practice of Tibetan Buddhism, a discipline Glass began studying almost thirty years ago. Glass says that hardly a day goes by when he is not aware of the impact that Buddhist meditation has had on him.

"I start the day with a program of Buddhist meditative practice, which can take a little bit of time, and along with it a very thorough exercise program. People always say, 'Wouldn't it be better to sit down and just start working?' But at the end of that preparation, when I sit down to work, I feel extremely focused. My body is prepared to sit comfortably for a fairly extended time, and I'm not distracted. This kind of preparation makes it possible to work with a very high degree of concentration in a fairly effortless way. In order to work for ten or twelve hours at a stretch, you have to be relaxed about it. You can be concentrated, but the effort can't prevent you from working."

From the outset, Glass's exposure to music had an

emphasis on that which was not commercially viable. Perhaps there is some connection between the fact that much of his music is considered "challenging" and the fact that it was only those albums that were unpopular and did not sell in his father's Baltimore record shop that the young Glass heard at home. While his father listened to them and tried to figure out why they didn't appeal to customers, Glass got an education in Shostakovich symphonies and Schubert sonatas. After trying violin at the age of six, Glass picked up the flute at eight and began an extremely disciplined relationship with music that continues to this day. At the age of fifteen he was accepted into the University of Chicago, where he majored in mathematics and philosophy. Both areas of study would have a major impact on his music.

After graduation he moved to New York and entered Juilliard, where he abandoned the twelve-tone techniques then dominant among American composers. Rejecting serialism, he moved to Paris, where he managed to get work on a film set to earn cash. As it turned out, the movie was *Chappaqua*, a counterculture film with a score by Ravi Shankar, and director Conrad Rooks hired Glass to transcribe Shankar's complex melodies for the bewildered French studio musicians who were recording the score. It was an enlightening experience for Glass, who discovered that the Indian tonal system did not divide music the way Western notation does, but instead adds to it. The insight that Glass derived from the Eastern approach to music not only changed the course of his own work but also had an impact on the general direction of contemporary classical music.

Returning to New York in 1967, Glass entered a frantically productive period, and he hasn't really let up since. He cofounded the Mabou Mines Theater Company

and composed a large body of music for the troupe to perform; he founded his own group, the Philip Glass Ensem-
ble; and he wrote *Music in Twelve Parts*, a four-hour piece
in which his musical ideas were fully realized. Those ideas,
which he has continued to mine in subsequent work, were
characterized by a relentless pulse that seemed to have
more to do with rock than with classical music or opera; by
harmonies that remained unchanged for long periods of
time, recalling the long, droning music of LaMonte Young;
and by short loops of repetitive melodies typical of minimalism. But although Glass's music may seem deeply repetitive, if you listen carefully, even his early works reveal
a multitude of subtly shifting tonal colors and melodic
statements.

In 1976 the French secretary of state for culture,
Michel Guy, commissioned Glass to compose the seminal
opera *Einstein on the Beach*. Created in collaboration with
Robert Wilson, *Einstein* catapulted Glass to new levels of
public recognition, while earning him both acclaim and
scorn from critics. Many found his simplicity and repetition insulting: Glass's radical austerity, as *Rolling Stone*
noted, struck some listeners as a way of "thumbing its nose
at every other music of the day, both classical and popular."

Although money began flowing in, the cost of producing mixed-media operas was immense—despite sellout
audiences, *Einstein*'s tour of the United States ran up a
$100,000 deficit. In 1977 Glass still had to work as a taxi
driver to pay the bills. But his output as a composer continued to be prodigious and, while never straying too far
from the essential structures of minimalism, continued to
expand in ever more sumptuous ways. "I just couldn't
throw out my Western music and education entirely," he
told *Time* magazine in a 1985 profile. Today he does not

consider himself a minimalist, and his recent work has gone far past the severities that the term once connoted.

Glass is so prolific, even a short list of his accomplishments would include several symphonies, string quartets written for the Kronos Quartet, a ballet for La Scala, the scores to films by Godfrey Reggio, and collaborations with figures as diverse as choreographer Twyla Tharp, director Paul Schrader, and playwright David Henry Hwang. A wide range of artists have inspired his music: he has created work based on the music of David Bowie, the poems of Allen Ginsberg, a story by Edgar Allan Poe, a novel by Doris Lessing, and three films by Jean Cocteau.

If any one particular tradition has become painfully trendy of late, it's Tibetan Buddhism, but there are a few prominent names in the circle of Buddhist musicians who are recognized even by Tibetan lamas for the seriousness of their study. Glass is one of them. For Glass, the tranquillity and clarity that meditation provides are essential to his life as a composer, and Buddhist philosophy and psychology inform his understanding of the world around him. "In life we face tremendous hardships. Unhappiness is just built in, and a lot of it is caused by our own delusions. By delusions, I mean that we just don't see the world the way it really is. We're worried about things that aren't real. If we examine it closely, we find that we cause our own unhappiness. The practice of meditation is to remove the delusions, to calm the mind and bring it to a less agitated state so we can think more clearly about what's going on. The other thing is to try to change to a less self-oriented point of view. When we begin to do that, a lot of our unhappiness is alleviated.

"These are the Buddha's four noble truths: the fact of suffering, the causes of suffering, the cessation of suffering, and the way to do it. We can't do any better than that."

The particular school of Buddhism that evolved in Tibet, known as Vajrayana, emphasizes complex visualizations. Esoteric, ornate, and vibrant, these traditions of meditation require a disciplining of the imagination, which appeals to Glass for some of the same reasons it might appeal to any individual whose creative work requires single-pointed mental focus. But beyond the benefits of improved concentration, Glass does not think there is any definite relationship between his meditative practice and his creative process as a composer.

"Meditation is a very complicated thing. A lot of people think it means sitting still and thinking about nothing, and there is meditation like that, meditation that calms the mind. But there's also meditation that trains the mind, or retrains the mind, so that we think in a different way. This type of meditation is a way of reforming our mental processes, in a way.

"With regard to the relationship between creativity and meditation, the fact is that people have been creative for forty or fifty thousand years, most of them without practicing any formal meditation. If you tried to find out whether Rembrandt or Schubert meditated, you might not find any formal sign of it. You might find it in John Cage, but he's more contemporary. I don't think it's easy to pin down the relationship between the two."

Where Glass sees a clearer relationship is between the tenets of Buddhism and his motivation as a musician. Buddhist doctrine stresses the value of decreasing others' suffering, so to the degree that music offers people relief from their pain and stress, from a Buddhist point of view, the life of a musician is a noble pursuit. By developing an altruistic motivation, one transforms a career in music into spiritual practice. "What the Dalai Lama emphasizes is kindness, compassion, and overcoming negativity. If someone asked, what is the basic practice of Buddhism, I'd say it is overcoming negativity. And I can think of nothing negative about music. People love music. It is very nourishing because it takes people out of their everyday mentality and brings them to another level. Making people happy becomes the motivation for the music.

"For a Buddhist practitioner, being a musician is almost the best thing. Of course, as a business, music is very complicated and it can be very adversarial, but you can learn to see things from a less self-centered point of view, which is what causes all the trouble. Why isn't my name biggest on the poster? Why isn't my dressing room the biggest? Where's my limo? If you're in the misery of self-absorption, there's no way you can be free to see things objectively. You do have to stand up for the work because you want it to be successful, but it doesn't have to be about self-grasping.

"Why are we writing a piece of music? Why are we making a record? Motivation counts for a tremendous amount, and considering your motivation at the beginning of each day is one of the main practices. As students of Gelek Rinpoche, one of the things we are taught is to dedicate our work. In other words, you dedicate the work for the benefit of other people. If you begin every concert with that dedication, in fact, if you can begin every day that way, slowly it begins to reform the way you work. It also relieves you of a kind of self-involvement, which is not particularly constructive in creative work, you know, the kind of vanity, self-absorption, and careerism that we see a lot of in the music business.

"When you dedicate the work and think of it as benefiting other people primarily—of course, you have to make a living, too—then it really works to take the focus off yourself, which is very liberating. It frees you from all kinds of problems. If you get a good review or a bad review, you simply say, Well, I didn't write this music for the reviewer alone, or even for myself alone. This way negative reaction to your works becomes less hurtful and the praise doesn't make you lose your ability to criticize yourself. So for a number of reasons, setting the motivation for the work and dedicating it to the happiness of others is very important. Now, what does this have to do with meditation? Well, you can meditate on motivation; there are very powerful techniques for concentrated meditation on a given subject, and motivation can be one of them.

"This is a way to restructure the way we work. For me, that's the most important thing. It's interesting to think of meditation as a way to make the mind more creative, and that may be true, but I'm not interested in that question right now. I'm really interested in motivation and how we work, particularly in relation to other people."

While it is true that by shifting one's motivation from self-obsession toward altruism, an artist may experience freedom from certain self-imposed constraints, there is also a commonly held belief that artists need a certain degree of self-obsession in order to work, that great art may require a big ego and perhaps a lot of neurosis. As a result, many artists fear that sanity, moderation, or happiness would destroy their work. "There are many stories about crazy artists, and the stories may be true, but they lead to a kind of indulgence. People say, 'Well, Picasso was an outrageous character and he was a great painter,' and they use that to justify their behavior. But that's pretty lame, isn't it? I don't think we have to link psychological or emotional anxiety with creativity. That's a Freudian idea, the whole idea of the sublimation of our problems in art. That's a particularly Western and modern idea and I don't know whether it's true. If you look at Bach's life, he didn't seem to be crazy, yet I can't think of anyone who was more creative. We have plenty of counterexamples of very creative people who lived in an emotionally wholesome way. The idea that creativity has to be linked with a negative personality structure is a bunch of baloney.

"The creative process is a current of thought that seems to inform and activate the work that we do, but it's very hard to find the source of that current, very hard to monitor it, very hard to control it. My own experience is that it seems to be totally independent of whatever I might do or be experiencing. People ask how Mozart could write such happy music at a time when he was so miserable. I think it's because the current of creativity operates on a level that is quite different from personality. It's almost an organic mechanism that is beyond conscious reach. For example, I've noticed that my physical fatigue has very little effect on the quality of the work that I do. Let's say I don't sleep much one night and I have to get up and work all day. The quality of the work will be the same, it's just that I'm kind of miserable.

"The current of creativity operates beyond our conscious mind, and we have very little access to it. If we're lucky, it's a very active part of our life. How do we make it more active? I have no idea at all. In my own case, I provided myself with the kind of musical training and background that would be necessary to do the work I'm doing, but I'm not sure it had much to do with the creative activity itself. I think that the development of my musical language seems to go along by itself, no matter what I do. I bring to bear my intellectual and technical abilities, but the actual creative process is full of surprises, and I have very little insight into how it works."

While Glass doesn't claim that meditation has helped him to gain insight into the creative process itself, he is very clear that it has penetrated his experience as a composer and performer. "It certainly makes our work easier when we begin to understand how our minds operate, how we and other people create delusions, misperceptions, and projections unceasingly. For example, if I hear that someone doesn't like my music, I understand that they're not hearing what I'm hearing, or not hearing it in the same way. There's a whole system of Buddhist psychology that helps us see that we all operate in the same deluded way, which helps us take the world less personally. It helps us understand that things aren't really directed at us: people are acting out their own delusions and fantasies and we just happen to be in the way. The other side of it is that I can see that the work I do functions in the world in a very real way, that people listen to the music and get different kinds of pleasure from it.

"When we talk about Buddhist psychology, we're not talking about some kind of New Age business. Buddhist psychology has been around for a couple of thousand years, and an understanding of egolessness and self-cherishing, of the aggregates that create the personality, of how the mind works, makes the world seem a little more reasonable."

JOAN OSBORNE
Transcendent Pleasure As Prayer

There is a saying in the music industry: for a long time, everything happens too slowly, then, when success hits, everything happens too fast. In Joan Osborne's case, this is especially apt. For years she paid to play, booking her own gigs, licking stamps herself for the flyers she sent to her mailing list, calling friends to come out and see her, hauling gear, and generally struggling in the fun but furiously competitive New York City club scene of the late eighties and early nineties.

Most of the music that was being played in New York City at the time was a combination of art-damaged funk and blues-rock that appealed to kids who had just gotten out of college, people who were tired of jangly rock but weren't ready to give themselves fully to the emergent hip-hop scene. Bands on this circuit included the Spin Doctors, the Surreal McCoys, Milo Z, Blues Traveler, plus lots of other groups people have never heard of because they gave up, broke up, or continued to struggle in near anonymity. It was a brutal crucible and still is. In New York City bands have to pay high rents for rehearsal space, pay for cabs to move their equipment, and sometimes even pay clubs for the opportunity to play. Musicians' friends have to pay exorbitant amounts to get in the door. And in a city with a thousand live-entertainment options every night, and several thousand heavily armed incentives to stay

home after dark, the competition makes it seem almost not worth it.

If there is a good thing about the New York music scene, it's that the weak die off quickly, and any act that lasts five years, to paraphrase Nietzsche, must be fairly strong by virtue of not being dead.

Joan Osborne was one of those acts. She had no money, no friends in powerful places, and no particular shtick. She had a voice, though, and she had endurance. Night after night, year after year, Osborne played the same circuit, mainly to the same crowd of faces. There was no sign that all her dues-paying would ever pay off.

Then, as suddenly as sudden can be, success hit. After playing a gig in Philadelphia in 1993, she got a call from a producer named Rick Chertoff, whose major claim to fame had been producing the forgettable eighties power-pop outfit the Hooters. Osborne was initially suspicious of Chertoff and what she may have perceived as his uncool musical associations, but a conversation convinced her there might be some point in negotiating with him—especially since he was looking for an artist to launch his new label, Blue Gorilla.

A deal was worked out, and although the resulting album, 1995's *Relish*, didn't showcase much of the grit of Osborne's Joplinesque live shows, it earned her seven Grammy nominations, the cover of *Rolling Stone*, appearances on Letterman, Leno, and *Saturday Night Live*, month-long blanket exposure on VH-1 as artist of the month, joint appearances with the likes of Stevie Wonder, Peter Gabriel, Nusrat Fateh Ali Khan, the Who, Michael Stipe, Don Henley, and others, as well as raves from magazines like *Entertainment Weekly* (which called *Relish* the best album of the year).

The irony of this deluge of fame is that it was largely

brought on by the song "One of Us," which was the only cut on *Relish* that Osborne had no part in writing. The song, which Osborne sings in an uncharacteristically child-like voice, asks a simple question: "What if God was one of us? Just a slob like one of us. Just a stranger on the bus." Its melody, a mournful, elemental crawl, was burned into the popular consciousness by heavy rotation on MTV and rock radio from New York to London.

The story goes that while Osborne was in the process of recording *Relish*, Eric Brazilian, the former Hooters guitarist who played on and cowrote most of the album, brought in a crappy little cassette recording of "One of Us" that he had dashed off the night before. He said he wrote the song merely as fodder to show his girlfriend how his home studio worked. "When Eric came in one morning and played us his version of 'One of Us,' there was a lot of processing of the vocals. It was very dirgelike and it sounded very much like a Leonard Cohen sort of song. He played it for us to just sort of get our feedback on it, saying, 'This is something that I want to do for my solo album that I might do someday.' Then the producer, Rick, heard it and was, like, 'Wow, let's hear it again—that's really kind of a cool song. Joan, why don't you try singing that?' And I did. Eric played it on the guitar, and for whatever reason, I just started to do it in this really simple, clear tone of voice. They made a recording of it and we played it back. I think Rick was probably the person it dawned on first, because that's his job, you know, determining what is a hit song and what isn't a hit song. He was, like, 'You know— this is a hit song!' To me it just seemed this odd, weird little thing, and I thought, 'Well, I don't know, I'm not sure you're right about it.' I mean, I liked it—I liked the way it sounded very innocent. It was like a little kid asking you a question, tugging on your sleeve, and you maybe don't listen to it at first, but then, a few minutes later, you start thinking about the question the kid's asking, and it's a very deep question."

Some people didn't like the way the question was asked, or the song's radically populist, nearly pantheistic message. Perhaps it was the assertion that God could be the smelly guy next to you on the bus that irked religious conservatives. In any event, "One of Us" landed Osborne on the cover of the *New York Post*, with a tabloid headline asserting, CATHOLICS CALL GRAMMY STAR'S SONG A DISGRACE. Reaction within the church has by no means been uniform: Osborne has been assailed by conservative evangelists and offered free Bible lessons, but she has also had a number of requests to sing for Sunday schools. As Osborne told *Out* magazine, "Maybe I address spirituality in nontraditional ways, but I don't make music in order to pick fights with the Catholic Church. Besides, the church's stands on homosexuality and women make the pope look far more ridiculous than any pop song could."

Controversy or not, without "One of Us," chances are that Osborne would still have earned a lot of respect for her singing, and surely critics would have taken notice of her fine songwriting. But it is unlikely that she would have become the recognizable artist she is today. The rest of the album was more typical of Osborne: lustful, sybaritic, thoughtful, and gushing with emotion. The lyrics reflected an eye for detail that brought everyday experiences to life with uncanny clarity. In one tune, "Right Hand Man," she describes the feeling of elation that accompanies leaving a man's apartment after a one-night stand. With her "panties crumpled in a ball at the bottom of her purse," she struts up the avenue, knowing that the men leering at her can sense the smell of sex and the air of satisfaction she's exuding at that particular moment.

But Osborne's songwriting is more than just a cataloging of sensual experiences; her overriding concern seems to be the redemptive power of pleasure. She portrays Eve as the inventor of kissing in "Lumina," and in "St. Theresa" she sings about a sanctified prostitute. Unlike Janis Joplin, to whom she is often compared, Osborne does not have a self-destructive bent. And unlike Joplin, or almost any other female rocker, she's not reticent about calling herself a feminist. Osborne wore a pro-choice T-shirt when she appeared on *Saturday Night Live*, and until her touring schedule made it impossible, she worked as an escort for women at a New York abortion clinic. While Osborne knows her Germaine Greer from her Betty Friedan, she's not particularly interested in lecturing people about feminism. She's too focused on the transformative power of music to marginalize her message with bloodless theorizing. As she told *Rolling Stone*, "I would like to promote a certain kind of positive, sexy, real, funny, image."

Osborne grew up in the small town of Anchorage, Kentucky. The Anchorage Osborne knew as a child wasn't as culturally isolated as some parts of the rural deep South. "I wouldn't say it was backwater. It was relatively sophisticated for that part of the country. Anchorage was kind of its own small town, and then, as the city of Louisville got bigger and bigger, it ended up being almost like a bedroom community for Louisville."

Her father was a general contractor. Her mother worked occasionally as an interior decorator. There was always food on the table, but because there were six children in the family, money was never in great abundance. The family attended Catholic masses while Osborne was still a young child, but eventually her father became disillusioned and refused to attend services. "My parents were

Catholic and that was very much a part of their life. It was what their social world centered around, and so we went to church from our young childhood up until I was about nine years old. I didn't really learn about this till later, I only sort of intuited it at the time, but my father sort of had a falling out, either with specific people in the church or just with the whole idea of it. He felt there was a lot of hypocrisy going on and that he could no longer go to church, so he stopped going." Osborne's mother continued trying to bring the family to church by herself, but the sheer physical strain of dressing, transporting, and chaperoning six children overwhelmed her, and eventually the family stopped going altogether.

From a very young age, Osborne experienced a pining for some sort of direct, transcendent connection with God. "I was pretty fascinated with the church experience and with the church itself. I would sometimes go back in after the mass was over. I'd just stand at the back of the church, and I thought I could see Jesus walking around behind the altar. I could see a shadow or something and thought that must be Jesus." Although this might be partly written off as the product of a young girl's overactive imagination, it was an experience that had a profound effect on her thinking as she grew up, and later, on her songwriting. "Even as a child it was obvious to me that there was something different about the physical building of the church itself. I think I was fixated on that as a special place. I felt that you changed when you went in there, and when you came out again, you changed back."

Although Osborne has had a strong faith in God for as long as she can remember, she is at a loss to define exactly what that God means. "It's so funny to say you believe in God, or you don't believe in God. I think everyone's definition of that is so varied that when you say that, you might mean one very specific thing and you're going to get about fifty thousand different interpretations of what you've just said. I think that when I was younger, it was more a belief in the Jesus that I saw in the pictures on the wall, and in the stained glass windows, and the Jesus I imagined I saw walking around behind the altar. But as I've gotten older, it's become less specific than that—it's more just an awareness of the miraculous nature of ordinary things. And a belief in God that comes from that."

Osborne's interest in religion has always tended toward those traditions that emphasize transcendent experience. And although she left the Catholic Church as a child, she has remained fascinated by the more esoteric forms of Christianity, the Coptics, the snake handlers, and the deep southern Baptists. And she has traveled as far as Lahore, Pakistan, to be initiated into the ecstatic Sufi tradition of qawwali singing.

These days she's not a regular churchgoer, but even now, when the chance arises, she'll duck into a church and sit down in the pews for a few minutes. "Once in a while I still go to church just because I love the atmosphere inside a church; it's a very beautiful place. If you live in New York City and you walk in off the street—you find a church and go inside—it's a really quiet, beautiful, contemplative place, whether there's a mass going on or not.

"I don't really consider myself a Catholic. I have a lot of problems with the institution of the Catholic Church and the political stance that it takes, and I feel it would be sort of insincere of me to take a part in mass and go to church every Sunday, because when you start connecting yourself with this huge monolithic institution, that's a bit of a lie. The most spiritual moments that I have are generally when I'm by myself."

After her family stopped going to church, Osborne

continued to pray, although in general her moments of contemplation were not prayer in the sense of supplication. In fact, most often prayer was something that came upon her rather than an act that she intentionally undertook. "I would spend a lot of time off in the woods walking around and sort of daydreaming. And sometimes that kind of thought would slip into something like a prayer, but more like a speculation about the nature of certain things. Questions about the nature of the love that people have for each other. I guess I saw that as almost a physically quantifiable thing, almost like weight and mass. Like, what does the love that all of us feel for each other, all around the world, add up to? I guess I saw love as this blanket wrapping around the world. So my 'prayers' were more like thinking about these sorts of spiritual and mystical things, kind of pointing to them and just playing with them in my mind, and not even necessarily wanting something and praying to get it. It wasn't that I felt myself distanced from God and was trying to get closer to him somehow, or anything like that. It was really just kind of walking around in this room that was my mind and picking things up and examining them. Sort of exploring your own thoughts.

"I've done some yoga and meditation and things like that, just things I've picked up from books and I've felt that can be really effective for focusing my mind and my energy, whether it's a task that I'm trying to do or an awareness of myself in the world at large. But I haven't ever had any kind of guru or teacher."

In the visualizations she sometimes practices, Osborne sits down and imagines a figure in front of her; from the being's forehead she visualizes a glow coming toward her. The glow reaches across and touches her on her forehead and she begins to feel a golden, nectarlike warmth

filling her head, infusing it with energy, healing every cell
in her. Then she imagines another glow in the throat of
the figure and pictures it coming toward her throat and
surrounding her vocal cords with warmth and filling them
with light.

Osborne's earliest memory of vocal training is of
wandering off in the wooded areas near her hometown
and engaging in a call-and-response with the birds. "I
started singing at a very, very young age. Anchorage was a
pretty small town, with a lot of woods, horse trailers, things
like that. I used to go into the yard and try to sing to the
birds. I could tell they were singing to each other when
they were sitting in the trees. So I would do little birdcalls
and try to imitate—not in a birdcall sort of way, not like
literally imitating them—but I would try to sing to them
in a way that they would somehow hear it and sing back
to me."

She enjoyed whatever musical experiences she
stumbled upon, but as a child she never thought about
having a career in music. Osborne was never formally
trained as a singer and did not initially have any sense of
herself as being particularly gifted in that area. "I used to
sing in church with everyone else, even though I didn't
always know what I was singing. As a little kid, I couldn't
read music, so I used to open up the hymnbook and try to
sing what everyone else was singing and go along with
that. No one ever sat us down and taught us how to do it,
so I just tried to sing along and do the best I could. I remember once, in school, just singing in the chorus, and I
really loved that; there was a real feeling of freedom because I could do a lot of things with my voice. I could sing
all the high parts, I could sing all the low parts, I had a
very elastic voice. I wasn't even really conscious of it at the
time, I just figured anyone could do this and that singing

was just a cool, fun thing where you could make your voice do all these wild things. I didn't realize until a little later that maybe I could do more than other people, because a music teacher of mine started focusing attention on me, having me sing solos, complimenting me, and working with me after school. I sort of thought it was this thing like breathing, that anyone could do, but I just really enjoyed it."

Osborne's debut as a rock singer could not have been less auspicious: in 1979 she sang a few cheesy covers with her boyfriend's high school band, before she was unceremoniously kicked out of the group because of jealousy on the part of another band member. "I came to music kind of late as a career, even though I had a real passion for singing as a kid. I thought maybe I'd be a scientist. I got good grades in school, you know, top of the class in tenth grade and all that. I think my parents wanted me to be a lawyer or a doctor, and I thought I wanted to be an archeologist or a marine biologist. And then I went to college in Kentucky, the University of Louisville. I took a couple of theater courses; I got really interested in that and the whole process of telling a story—not so much as performer but as a director or writer. And then I looked around and realized that pretty much no one in this country goes to the theater. So if you wanted to tell stories in that way, you would have to take a more democratic art form, and I thought that film would be really interesting to pursue."

In the fall of 1982, Osborne moved from Kentucky to New York City and enrolled at New York University. She had never been in a band for any length of time and still had no intentions to pursue music. "I didn't even have a stereo or a radio when I went to film school at NYU. I was putting myself through school, and I did that for three years. I had to take six months off at one point and go back home to Kentucky to earn some more money to go back again. I had a couple of scholarships, but I also worked at two different jobs the summer before to save money, and I was just really, really poor. I literally didn't have enough money to take the subway, so I would walk home at night by myself, and I would eat a bagel and cream cheese and an apple and that would be my meal for the day. I was living on thirty-five dollars a week. I lived first in the YMCA on Thirty-fourth Street and Ninth Avenue, in one of those little rooms, it was just really awful, roach infested. I mean, I would wake up and there would be roaches on my face in the morning; it was just really terrible. And then I went to a place in Brooklyn, it was a tiny little room. I didn't know anyone, and I met people at school and made some friends there, but I really was pretty much alone and very broke when I came to New York.

"The reason I first started singing was that I lived in an apartment where there was a blues bar on the corner. It was called the Abilene Café, on Twenty-first Street and Second Avenue. One night this guy who lived in my building said, 'Let's go get a beer down at this place on the corner, it's really cool.' So he took me there and it was really late, it was like two o'clock in the morning or something, and the band had finished their sets and were pretty much done for the night. But there was this one guy still up there, and my friend said, 'You know, I heard you singing to the radio and you sounded really good. I dare you to go up and sing a song with him right now.' There was pretty much nobody in the place, maybe five or ten people just hanging around, drinking. So I did. I sang Billy Holiday's 'God Bless the Child.' There was something about standing next to the piano, singing this really intense song, and then having it be in something of a public spot, that really, really shook me. I think it partly had to do with the fact that what I had been doing up until then, working in film, was much more of an intellectual process. Performing is more about your body and your emotions; especially singing, it's about your breathing. It can really take hold of every part of you—not only your intellect and your emotions but your body and your soul as well. The work I had been doing with film was much more about technique and intellect, and I just feel like there had been this whole part of me that had been sort of neglected or cut off. And so I think that's why I reacted so strongly to singing that night at the bar. The piano player said, 'That sounded really nice. Why don't you come to our open jam nights that we have here once a week?' So I started going to these open-night things and I would sing one or two songs. I would go out and buy a few blues records that week—by this time I had a stereo—and learn a few cool songs, and then I would go up and sing two songs and that would be my turn. I would hang out in the club all night long, waiting for my turn to come, talking to the people, listening to the other musicians who were doing their little jam.

"Singing there had a real hold on me. Even though I was kind of nervous and scared of doing it in front of people, it just struck me in this way that kept me coming back. And there was also this community of musicians, which was kind of fascinating to me. I was just as much a fan of other people's music as I was involved in doing it myself, so my singing was a way for me to be part of this community, and I think that was really what kept me doing it. And it just grew little by little. I was able to put together a band of my own, doing gigs. We started out doing gigs in one or two clubs, and then it was five or six or seven clubs. I started thinking maybe this could be something I could do for a living, and that if I treated it like a business, we would be able to put out records, have a following and have it grow slowly, and that maybe eventually it might turn into being a national recording act or whatever.

"There was this one guy who was a fan and would come to all the shows, and he said that if we ever needed any money, he'd be willing to invest in our band. So we took him up on it. He gave us, like, ten thousand dollars to do the first CD that we did in 1991."

The first CD Osborne released, on her own Womanly Hips label, was called *Soul Show: Live at Delta 88*. It was essentially a live recording of a decent bar band walking through standard Memphis and honky-tonk jams. Osborne is the only thing that makes it interesting—a noticeably gifted vocalist exploring the limits of her voice. Her performance is more nuanced than any of the original songwriting, but the group's next effort, an EP called *Blue Million Miles*, found Osborne stretching her limits as a writer, breaking out of the confines of bluesy bar rock. "I used to write just as a way of understanding things for myself. I think there was something that compelled me to write down an experience or describe something very specifically, maybe so I could understand it. There was something about the act of capturing an experience or a feeling in words that I always used to come back to. I used to keep journals or write letters or whatever, so writing was always a part of my life; it just didn't become songs until much later."

When *Relish* came out, Osborne's nearly cinematic eye for detail drew much attention from record reviewers, most of whom assumed it was a reflection of her background as a student filmmaker. In fact, she had been honing her descriptive skills for years, jotting down notes and rendering in painstaking detail those events and people whose vividness impressed themselves upon her. Whereas when most people write in journals, they record their emotions or explore their poetic sides, Osborne's writing always leaned toward objective, journalistic observation. Speaking of the pages that filled her early journals, she says, "They were about sitting on a bench at a bus stop and having some person sit next to me who was unusual in some way and just trying to describe exactly what it was that was unusual about that person. Or if I'm walking down the street and some redneck in a pick-up truck leans his head out the window and screams at me, what does that feel like? It was more like an examination of the world around me."

Osborne's examinations were by no means limited to the world around her: she also turned the flashlight inward, discovering ecstatic revelatory states that seemed to arise spontaneously in her mindstream. "I do recall having, not necessarily a religious experience, but . . . one night that I remember was in college, it was probably late in 1980, I'd just gone to see some movie and I was walking home alone and got this feeling, almost like a pang of joy. I didn't know what it was connected to; there was no sudden realization of some amazing truth or anything like that, it was just this incredible feeling of elation. And I started walking around in this neighborhood that I lived in and I ended up climbing on top of this building and just lying there looking at the stars and just feeling this. It lasted for hours and hours and I don't know why it happened. That's happened to me a few times in my life, where I just get this overwhelming sense of elation and joy. I don't really know what it means or what it's connected to, and I'm not really questioning it or asking why it's happening or anything like that. It's almost like I've stumbled onto this weird corridor of energy and have been caught in it.

"It really manifests itself in a very physical way.

When I'm onstage and I start to get that feeling, I stop thinking about what I'm doing and I stop being so aware of myself, the audience, or of standing in front of people. A lot of times when I'm onstage, I'll get covered in goose bumps. I'll start to feel this pleasure in just breathing, and the singing is suddenly completely effortless. I've had ecstatic experiences like that—well, not ecstatic, I wouldn't say that—but that sort of totally pleasurable thing, as if I were taking drugs or something. It's really a physical thing. I guess it's sort of similar to a sexual response too, because its very much something I feel in my skin and all up and down my body. That happens a lot—that's more like the garden-variety experience. But then I've had experiences where I'll be looking up at a light that's pointing toward the stage and then suddenly everything around that light will look completely dark and it's almost like there's this tunnel and it's just the light and me, and that's all I'm really aware of, just this incredibly pleasurable moment. But I don't see the Virgin Mary or anything like that; it's never a specific religious thing. It's really just a kind of physical manifestation and a rush of joyous feeling."

Although these experiences are not something that Osborne works at or cultivates, and she has not been struggling to perfect them or increase them in any way, she still views the experience in the context of a certain kind of musical/spiritual discipline, akin to the tradition of gospel. "It's almost like it's this random, spontaneous thing— because of what I do for a living and because this music that I'm drawn to is a very expressive music, coming from a whole tradition of worship and gospel and trying to connect the self with something larger than the self. I think that is a discipline in itself. But I don't consciously bring it on. I mean, the reason I started singing was that it felt very

pleasurable and was a very emotional, cathartic experience, but not like, 'Oh, I'm venting my emotions now and
I feel cleansed by it.' There was also a feeling that music is
this huge stew that you and everyone who's listening to it
are floating around in. So it's a personal thing and it's an
expressive thing, but it also feels like you're rising above
your own self and your own person and being part of
something larger—one of those moments when everything
else disappears and it's just this pleasurable kind of thing."

Transcending the limitations of the self and com-
muning with something larger is, in Osborne's view, not
only a pleasure but a responsibility that comes with the gift
of musical talent. She believes that in order to fully realize
one's talent, to give full expression to it, some degree of
ego transcendence is necessary. "You're given some kind
of gift; it doesn't come *out* of you, it only comes *through* you.
It's not like you created yourself and made yourself into
this beautiful talent or whatever. You have to husband this
gift in a certain way and you have to treat it with respect,
but ultimately, it doesn't come from you, it comes from
somewhere else and you have to be able to realize this. You
need to share in some way. Making music is not really for
your own benefit, it is for the benefit of the people who are
listening. It's not about me and my personal emotion and
struggle, it's about trying to uplift the people who are
hearing it. The only moments when I have any doubts
about whether this is what I need to be doing in my life are
when I feel like it's egotistical for me to think that *I* am
doing that—like maybe having some video on MTV and
doing some stupid interview or whatever that has nothing
to do with anything and I'm just fooling myself. The only
moments of doubt that I've ever had about doing music
come when it becomes like going through the pop-culture
mill.

"I've never felt that what I do is about the ego gratification of having the people stand and watch me and listen to me. That's actually something that I was very uncomfortable with in the beginning and really didn't like so much—being very exposed and examined. I didn't want it that way. It was more about becoming a part of the music, of leaving part of the self behind and just becoming the song. There's this great line in a Chrissie Hynde song where she says, 'When I first heard a song flying to the sun, I wanted to be one.' You know, it's not that you want to sing the song, it's that you want to be one."

ZIGGY MARLEY

Conscious Reggae from the Heir to the Throne

To paraphrase the great writer and gardener Jamaica Kincaid, traveling to a tropical island as a tourist inherently makes you ugly. As Kincaid pointed out in *A Small Place*, every native of the island would like to be a tourist, and every tourist is a native of some place. But every native wishes that he or she could be free from the tedium of life; to the tourist, the native's life is something to be observed, a form of entertainment. To the native, the tourist is an ugly reminder of being trapped.

In Jamaica you're made very aware of being an ugly tourist. In this place where the ugly tourist rubs the local's nose in the gap between rich and poor, Bob Marley, arguably the most famous entertainer ever to hail from a developing nation, helped to transform Rastafarianism—Jamaica's populist, underclass reinterpretation of the Bible—from a fringe social and religious movement into a widely accepted way of life. Before his death from cancer in 1981, Marley used reggae's pulsing meditative beat to carry a social and political message: the poverty of the underclass, the vagaries of ghetto existence, the politics of oppression. Marley couldn't change their economic condition, but he helped the poorest Jamaicans feel some pride, helped them not to feel like tourists in their own land.

In death, Bob Marley is what can only be described

as a semideity in Jamaica. Like Elvis Presley in America, Marley is seen by Jamaicans as much more than an entertainer: he is a religious figure, a social activist, and a manifestation of the island nation's spiritual and temporal potential, all rolled into one.

Ziggy Marley, Bob's oldest son, is heir to the Marley mystique. Like Julian Lennon, Nancy Sinatra, and Jakob Dylan, it would be impossible for Ziggy ever to live up to the legend of his father, but musically and philosophically, he knows exactly where he stands and where he's headed. "Success is spiritual enlightenment. The road I'm on now is to try to be successful in my own form of spirituality. When I reach that enlightened state, that is success," he says. "When I was a young kid, and they were comparing me to my father, I hadn't matured yet. They never waited, even though they hadn't seen the ripened fruit. It's still ripening."

In the house in Jamaica where Bob Marley lived, now a museum in his honor, is a small studio decorated with images of Bob and of His Imperial Majesty Haile Selassie, the late emperor of Ethiopia, who is believed by Rastafarians to be the Messiah. Ziggy Marley is listening to playbacks of "Born to Be Lively," a song from an upcoming album by his band, the Melody Makers; the tune features a marching hip-hop beat and lush vocals by Ziggy's sisters that recall the famous harmonies of the I-Threes, Bob's backup singers. One member of the I-Threes was Ziggy's mother, Rita Marley.

With a small crew of producers and engineers, Ziggy is discussing ways the beat could be varied. Ziggy and the Melody Makers have gone platinum a few times with American audiences, but they have more often failed in their attempts to find a commercially viable mix of reggae and pop. The next song they play back is "Melancholy

Mood," a hip-hop shuffle slowed to a NyQuil crawl. At around sixty beats per minute, it's about the slowest reggae track I've ever heard, with a mournful and sparse arrangement in marked contrast to the highly orchestrated pop for which the Melody Makers are known and sometimes criticized. Another cut, "Postman," a straight reggae number featuring younger brother Steven on lead vocals, sounds closer to Bob Marley than anything Ziggy and the Melody Makers have recorded. The song's chorus asks the question, "Are you getting Jah message?" It is, of course, a play on the words *the* and *Jah* (the latter being short for Jehovah), which is typical of the Rastafarian use of what is called word power. Word power involves integrating references to Rasta beliefs into everyday language; so, for example, to underscore the unity of all things, a Rasta might say "I and I" instead of "we."

The smell of marijuana permeates the small recording studio as Ziggy repeatedly ignites a spliff. Short, stocky and low-key, he has a soothing presence. He's calm, somewhat reserved, and has shiny, dark eyes that verge on inky blackness. During our interview, as we sat in a small room outside the studio, one of the power outages common in Kingston caused a blackout. As we sat in the darkness, the only light came from occasional flashes of those eyes, catching the red operating light from my battery-operated tape deck.

Marley's earliest memories of his spiritual life concern a dream he had as a young child, in which he saw Haile Selassie. "A dream that I remember from childhood was His Majesty in a big building walking down an aisle. That was how he first came to me, in a dream, like a vision. This was before I went to school or learned anything about Rasta."

Although Ziggy's father was the world's best-known

Rastafarian, Ziggy was not consistently exposed to the religion as a child. Born in humble surroundings in Jamaica ("in Trenchtown, on newspaper," his mother told *Vibe* magazine last year; "Bob was there, helping to clean up the blood"), he was sent to Delaware as a child, where he was raised by his grandmother. She regularly took Ziggy to a Baptist church, where his first exposure to formal religion was a world away from the mystical naturalism of Rasta. Ziggy doesn't feel that he chose to be a Rasta but that the Rasta way of life chose him.

"It just happened to me. It was a natural process— nothing planned, nothing forced. I believe it because I see it work in my life. I see the fulfillment of my faith because I see the reality of it affecting my life. Simple things. I see it is right because I have guidance from dreams and visions."

Ziggy read a variety of religious texts, including books of Buddhist dharma and the Koran. "From the time I was a youth, seeking knowledge was a part of my life. Reading books, seeking spirituality, trying to find the truth. I read everything because the Almighty revealed himself differently to different people. So it's not who you say you believe in but how you live. I don't care what religion you say you are if you're living right, living according to the natural laws of life."

Jamaican dancehall, the rapid-fire, patois cousin of hip-hop, often accompanied by staccato electronic drumbeats, is one of the musical styles young suburban teenagers can still rely on to irritate their parents. Even the coolest aging hippies and dyed-in-the-wool reggae fans are generally offended by records by Buju Banton, Super Cat, or Mad Cobra. Like rap, dancehall has been castigated for its "slack" lyrics. In reggae terminology, *slackness* refers to lyrics with violent or profane content, while "cultural," or "roots," reggae has a more positive, socially conscious message.

The title of Ziggy's 1989 breakthrough album, *Conscious Party*, made it clear that his loyalties were with roots reggae, although he has disappointed purists by experimenting with hip-hop, rhythm and blues, and other pop rhythms. "Roots is a foundation, the way it is meant to be. In life, Jah is the root. The tree grows up and branches out, but it is the roots that give it substance. So roots is very important to keep in music. If you lose the root, the tree dies."

When Ziggy talks about his faith in Rasta, it recalls the Chinese conception of the Tao—that we all have a natural path in life and the goal is to know who you are and be who you are. Other principles of his faith recall the Buddhist idea that all beings are born with Buddha nature, an innate wisdom and goodness. Although Rastafarianism is based on an interpretation of the Bible, this particular notion would appear to contravene the Christian idea of original sin.

"Jah creates human beings and we are naturally peaceful, are naturally loving. But through society and the system, things change. When you find that natural state of yourself, which is more than flesh, which is spiritual, then just be who you are. I and I deal with conscious living, because actions speak louder than words. Some prayer is important also, but your livity is the key—your living, your lifestyle. You can't just pray and live bad. Live good first.

"When I and I meditate, my mind is empty. The mind is not thinking of anything. It is not asking for anything. It's, like, it's everywhere, so, as they say, you are one with the universe. But we also pray as individuals. We ask Jah to guide us, to strengthen us, to protect us and other people."

Although there are formal Rastafarian organizations, Ziggy does not attend any church. "Just life. Our life is our church. The whole earth is Jah's church, and the heavens are the roof. We do have elders and patriarchs, men who have ancient wisdom—roots. That's why we talk about roots. That's important. Jamaica is full of mystics. They know the roots, and come from the roots, and are the roots."

When Ziggy was a child, he had his father as a teacher. Beyond that, he never had any specific religious instruction. "I didn't have anyone who gave me teachings, because life is a teaching. Action. Just how you live. I don't have to tell you the ABCs when I'm teaching about life. I don't have to tell you nothing. I just have to live the life that is clean and good and you'll see that. And that is your teaching. It's not what I say."

As a father Ziggy exhibits little of the introspection and reevaluation common among new parents. He believes in raising children by example. "My path is the path of livity. It's not self-enlightenment but self-awareness. That is my path. Nobody ever sat down and teach me this and teach me that. My path was searching and finding what is true. By studying and thinking and meditating, that was the way. So me no have no guru and no teacher."

Ziggy's stance isn't anti-intellectual (he is an avid reader), but he has a healthy working-class disdain for politicians, religious leaders, advertising executives, and other sources of big promises. The theme of hypocrisy is a constant in much of reggae's political expression: the mistrust of slick talkers, government, and the pleasant facade of big business.

The Rastafarian use of marijuana as a sacrament comes from an interpretation of a biblical admonition to partake of the herbs and seeds of the land. When Ziggy smokes marijuana, which is often, it is as a kind of lubrication for prayer or meditation. This is not without precedent in formal religion—Coptic Christians have won legal battles to include the use of marijuana in their services—but when weed is as ubiquitous as it is in the Jamaican music business, distinguishing between casual and prayerful use is difficult.

"When you are smoking herb you should read the Bible or study or meditate on the Creator. That's how I do it. And we do it when we play music, so we can meditate 'pon the music. That's why the music sounds too laid back! It's true that for some people it becomes a habit. Me, personally, I smoke plenty, plenty, but when me ready, I'll say, 'I'm not gonna smoke any today or tomorrow.' We are not preaching for everyone to smoke herb. But in my teachings and my roots, we always use herb. It's not the roots of everyone but it is part of the path that I have taken.

"Also, herb is a natural thing. We are against drugs like cocaine and alcohol and prescription drugs. I don't use aspirin. If I get sick, first thing I do is fast. Herb is like a medicine. When you take your medicine, you relax. If everyone smoked and got high, the place would be more lovely because everyone would be relaxed. If all the presidents and rulers of the earth smoked some herb, they'd be kicking back, saying, 'Yeah, mon, peace!'"

Ziggy has been fully initiated into the world of the Internet, engaging in cyberchats with fans and friends across the globe. His initial reaction was positive because he felt that being online, like making music, was an opportunity to tell the truth to many people. But before long his roots resurfaced and he became wary of those who go overboard with computers, losing touch with what he calls the natural laws of life.

"Technology is a thing you must not overuse because it sucks away your soul. Many people are getting hypnotized and highly addicted to this Internet thing. It's not good. You must keep your natural self at all times, your conscious self. If you get into that virtual world, you should always know that you can throw the computer away if you want, so you're not stuck. People think they're free because the authorities can't control the Internet. But it's like our album title says—*Free Like We Want 2 B*. I don't think we're free like we want to be. We're free to kill, free to hate—that's not the freedom we want."

Political consciousness seems to be a part of everyday life for many Jamaicans; it is not uncommon for people to slip casually from discussion of a soccer match to decrying the crimes of the military-industrial complex. Ziggy integrates his political views seamlessly into his life as an artist, having inherited not only his father's musical inclinations but also his proclivity toward social activism. "The whole society has to change, even the leaders have to change. They themselves have to show the people the love they want people to show each other. Mostly they are fighting wars right now. So where are they leading the people? To death. So these leaders are only bogus."

What role does Ziggy believe he can play as a musician to bring about change? "In a small way, touch who you can touch with music. You can only do what you can do. Yours is only a part to play."

When Ziggy talks about "the system" (or what some Jamaicans refer to as the shits-dem) it recalls an old-school preacher decrying the devil as an alien presence corrupting our original state of purity. "The system is dictating to the people. A lot of people can't relax because they want to buy a car or a house. That is the way the system wants it to be. What we call the system, the devil is into. This system is not something one man runs; it is a mentality, and this mentality is called Babylon. This mentally is called greed, oppression, the will to conquer. This is the way the world's zillionaires prosper."

Musicians who talk the talk about their devotion to social issues must answer the question, why, if they are so worried about less fortunate people, do they spend most of their time playing music? According to Ziggy, what makes the difference is what motivates you. "It doesn't matter what you are, if you's a doctor, a lawyer, a writer, a singer, a star—everyone have a purpose in life and that is to seek the Creator. But if you're seeking money, or if you're seeking fame, or if you're seeking sex, then that is a different path. When you are seeking the Creator, the road is clearer. Not easier, but it feels much better. By living that life you show each one so that they may follow you. So I don't feel no special way as a musician. I have a purpose as a musician because as a human being I have a purpose. As a man I have a purpose. As a creature of Jah I have a purpose: to seek the Creator. Seek Jah. Seek the truth. Seek the light. Seek the spiritual way. If all of us have that purpose, then we will all be more peaceful. We will be more loving to each other. There wouldn't be so much war, so much envy, so much greed.

"Let me tell you, music is a creation of the Almighty. Yeah. Ya know?' Cause music was before everything else. Before, there was a wind or the sound of a star moving through space; that is all natural music. So music not only speak from lyrics, but speak from itself—the spirit of the music itself. It's the vibes of the music itself speaking, different than the artist that's singing. Music have plenty power."

Marley confesses to the occasional guilty pleasure of listening to gangsta rap. Dr. Dre and Snoop get some play on the Marley hi-fi, but he considers himself "not hip" to the latest American music. For credibility in American dance clubs he relies on producers to remix his songs with the rhythms and styles popular in Atlanta, Chicago, Los Angeles, or New York. While he doesn't give his blessings to the negativity of some dancehall and rap, at least the gangsta rapper, he argues, is not a hypocrite. He emphasizes that big business often profits from the most violent strains of music. "The person that is doing the music, if he wants to approach a negative thing, then he approach it. But 'tis also the society and the system that causes all of these things and eventually promotes it, while denouncing it at the same time. It's money-making business even though the businessman says it's bad."

Notwithstanding that Ziggy is heir to one of the greatest fortunes ever amassed by an entertainer from a developing nation, the name of his record label is Ghetto Youth United. Ziggy certainly doesn't live in a ghetto, but he denies that his money has put up any barriers between him and the young Jamaicans who are his fans. "When I start making some money, I'll talk about that problem. Yeah, we make likkle dollars, do what we can, but I don't know about great billions and zillions. Just a small amount for me. That's all right. Money can never separate I from roots and culture, because I have the faith. Everything revolves around that. And there's nothing that can touch I, no envy, no greed. If I never have money, I still have to live, and Jah will provide if I don't provide. So those things never even get a chance to be planted as a seed. Me kill them before they're even planted."

Ziggy puts at least some of his money where his mouth is: part of the profits from 1995's "Hand to Mouth" were donated to the school where Ziggy and his siblings were educated. "We have so many dreams. We also want to build a school in Saint Thomas Parish. This is all a part of our work, and our spiritual work also, because we have to help our people."

As grounded as his music is in the Rasta tradition, Ziggy has no illusions about the fact that his career requires him to lead a fairly secular life. "I hope to gain more wisdom as the years go by because I know that at one point we will have to leave this world behind. And if I really wanted to attain the highest heights, I don't think I could spend my time touring and singing anymore."

This is an interesting admission, one that few musicians I interviewed for this book will cop to: that the life of the professional musician includes many hours of noncreative activity that make music as difficult to merge with a life of full spiritual practice as any other job.

"Not that I've given up, we keep on trying, but I know this for myself: that if you want enlightenment, you can't have another job, you have to be one hundred percent devoted. When you're on tour, there's more involved than just going onstage every night. Me can reach a level, but to reach that highest height, you need one hundred percent devotion. Just meditation and living good and helping people. But this is what Jah has given me to do. Until I reach that path, I'll continue on this one and do the best I can."

MICK JAGGER

The Rock Star As Catalyst

Two middle-aged Englishmen are sitting discussing what their next joint venture will be. One is interested in exploring interactive computer technology; the other prefers more familiar terrain. They have worked together for more than thirty years and are founders of a company that has made hundreds of millions of dollars.

Their names are Mick Jagger and Keith Richards, their company is called the Rolling Stones, and their business is rock and roll, which they have created, performed, and marketed with unrivaled endurance and success. They've been putting out hit records for three decades, and they recently finished a record-breaking world tour that brought in more than $300 million.

Jagger is a consummate professional, a performer whose concern with maintaining control is legendary. A graduate of the London School of Economics, he is keenly aware of the details of the Rolling Stones' business affairs. He has long been computer literate and was deeply involved with the planning and execution of the Stones' Web site. During a recent interview, dressed in a tweed jacket and sipping tea, Jagger looked more like a college professor than the man whose name has meant rock star for thirty years running.

Much of the mythology of contemporary rock and roll is based on the Stones' attitude and look circa 1968,

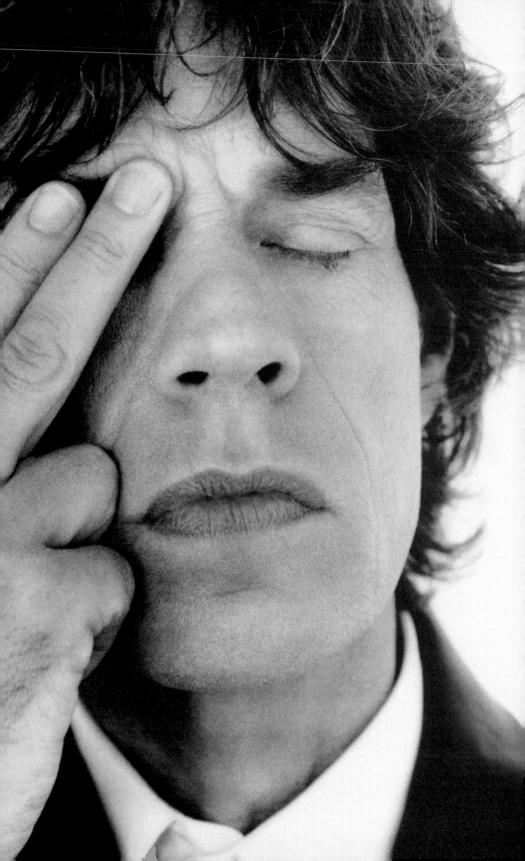

and it's easy to forget that in the late 1960s, Jagger and the rest of the Stones (along with many of their musical peers) were ridiculed as criminals, outcasts, and nuisances whose music and careers wouldn't last. Primal and shockingly handsome, Jagger was the satyr on acid, a skinny half-man/half-horse with mojo to spare. With his hint of eyeliner, studded wristbands, and dirt under his nails, he was the armchair anarchist who sang of good sex and fighting in the streets.

Now well into middle age, Jagger has cooled his interest in the music of the revolution and speaks of "evolutionary" social change, not street-fighting men. "I don't see rock and roll as a catalyst for revolution. Has rock and roll affected women's liberation? I have no idea. There are some postfeminist writers who talk a lot about rock music, so it seems to have affected them. Perhaps there's been an evolutionary change that rock and roll has been part of, but change happens even in the most terminal periods of stasis in a culture. You know, people always think of the fifties as the most static period, but the reality was very different. There was a genuine fuck-you attitude in the fifties and early sixties, and after that I think it just became a pose. It doesn't mean very much anymore because society has changed so much, but in the early, early days, there was a real statement to make.

"We didn't intend to shock people when we started out. We thought we were kind of normal. And then when we got to Texas we found out we weren't. Whereas now it's much more difficult to shock people. Although you want society to be more tolerant, you also want to do something that's slightly different, to be able to grab people's attention. When I was a teenager it was a real statement to do these things, whereas now it doesn't have any meaning.

There was a time when people were shocked by the lyrics of rap; now they don't seem to be shocked by anything.

"If you have something new to say, you get a reaction, like in the artistic movement that took place at the beginning of this century. There was a lot of music that people were shocked by: they would go to a concert and throw tomatoes at performers of the new atonal music. They would throw rotten fruit or riot. People got terribly upset and cut up paintings at the showings of Impressionist art at the salons of the nineteenth century. I suppose the only comparison we can make today is to how upset people got over Robert Mapplethorpe's photographs. But that was all over public money, it wasn't really over the pictures themselves—or at least, public money is what they said they were upset about."

Mick Jagger was there when something as simple as long hair was a snub to the established power structure, when people fought over the length of sideburns. Jagger was also there when rock and spirituality first crossed paths in a big way—the weekend in 1967 when he and John Lennon and George Harrison traveled out to Bangor, Wales, to meet Maharishi Mahesh Yogi. Although Harrison stayed on and became a disciple, Jagger only observed from a safe distance, more as a detached student than an acolyte. Jagger views the current interest among musicians in Eastern philosophy as a repetition of the same fin de siècle spiritual searching that marked the end of the nineteenth century.

"There's a hunger for spirituality," he says, "and the same rejection of Christian beliefs and search for other ways that happened at the turn of the last century. That makes me feel hopeful, because the beginning of the last century was actually very productive from an artistic point of view. There were a lot of new ideas burgeoning, and hopefully that may happen again. Of course, what followed all the new ideas was a very terrible war, so you don't want history to repeat itself. But I do think that the end of a century does undoubtedly produce something, and that's kind of exciting."

As Jagger looks forward, what he predicts isn't "only rock and roll," to paraphrase one of his song titles. "I think there's a lot happening in the visual arts, as there was at the beginning of this century. And visual arts now means film, TV, and computer-generated images, CD-ROM—anything you see. It doesn't have to be just a painting on a canvas, but it can include that."

With the exception of "Just Wanna See His Face," a moving hymn to Jesus, the Rolling Stones' body of recorded work has rarely strayed into the realm of explicit spirituality. But the band's best work has a sheer instinctive "rightness" to it, so much so that at times it isn't just right—it's righteous. The lesson of the Stones is in the band's delivery. For example, the song that completes one of their greatest albums, *Exile on Mainstreet*, is a stomping sped-up blues called "Soul Survivor." Listening to the track could help your soul survive, but the salvation wouldn't be in some literal message. It would be in the insistent sway of the rhythm, a groove played with such conviction that you could actually be affirmed by it. You could be uplifted by it. The gospel vocals that close the song amid a wash of testifying and glossolalia could make you feel like you were being carried aloft by a sea of sweaty hands and baptized. You can hear Jagger losing himself in the vocal performance.

"You do lose yourself," Jagger says of the experience of performing, "and when that transcendental moment happens, it can be quite scary. Because sometimes you lose yourself onstage and there are a lot of people out there. You can just get lost for whole moments, and I get scared when those moments happen. You wonder if you've been in that reverie too long. In jazz parlance they used to call it being gone. They'd say, 'He's gone.' "

The fact that Mick Jagger's name is inextricably linked with the idea of the iconic rock star makes it difficult to consider the individual behind the words. He is a slight man who moves gracefully and with a notable economy of motion, as though he were conserving his energy. That energy, which Jagger and the Stones have expended to such powerful effect on stage and records for so long now, is evident when we speak only in the glimmer of his eyes. (Keith Richards, on the other hand, would not easily be mistaken for an academic. A character driven more by instinct, he hasn't just immersed himself in the rock and roll lifestyle—he has lost himself in it.)

How is it possible that Jagger, so small in person, has not been bloated by playing the role of rock star for so long? How has he managed to stand in front of crowds of seventy-five thousand for so many years without becoming an egomaniacal monster? Mainly, he says, by recognizing that his success is based on a relationship between the Stones and their audience.

"You have to remember that you're only the catalyst for these events," Jagger says, "whether they're in a small club or at Giants Stadium. Though you might feel that the spotlight's on you, and physically it is, what's important is the relationship you're in with the audience. You're only the catalyst for this event in which people have come to one place and have been concentrating together to create some kind of feeling. It's the same feeling you get from going to a revival meeting, for example, the feeling that you're all there and you're sharing. So performing is an experience you share with the audience, and you lose your ego to some extent."

If performing for ecstatic crowds is a way to lose your ego, Jagger should be enlightened by now, because there are few people who've had as much practice as he has. In 1994, when the Rolling Stones began their seventeenth American tour, in Washington, D.C., I flew down from New York out of devotion to a band whose albums have been a part of my parents' household since before I was. But despite crystalline sound quality, a constantly jogging Jagger, and inspired song choices that reached back to the Rolling Stones' golden era, the sparks weren't flying.

I am perhaps an atypical fan in that I discovered early on that the Stones' magic is not the flashy, snarling persona of Mick Jagger nor the ominous, lazy playing of Keith Richards, but the brilliantly sloppy rhythm section of the band's Bill Wyman and Charlie Watts. But by the time of the Voodoo Lounge tour, in 1994, the Stones' live act was so tight it almost worked against them. The sound was so studio perfect one almost wondered whether they were lip-synching, and the drawback of such glossy production values was that the music no longer felt scary. The guitars weren't eerily out of tune anymore, as on some intoxicating bootlegs from the early seventies. Keith Richards and Ron Wood hardly ever started solos at the same time, as was their charming garage-band habit during much of the eighties. In short, the show came off without a hitch. And although Jagger could not be accused of skimping on the aerobic element—I began dancing at the beginning of a two-and-a-half-hour set and nearly had a heart attack trying to keep pace with him—the perfection of their stadium show threatened to turn the Rolling

Stones into a Las Vegas spectacle. Where was the famous satanic vibe?

"It's hard to get that sinister energy in a stadium," admits Jagger, "on the first night especially. You come to all that later. It's a real bust to play in these domes. I prefer to play in smaller venues, I hate these fucking stadiums."

Still, it was those "fucking stadiums" that earned the Rolling Stones $300 million for their most recent tour. Nobody can fault Jagger's performance in both dreaming up the creative side of the act and hiring the accountants who ensure that it's all so wildly profitable, but it is conceivable that money has corrupted him—and not just Jagger, but the entire idea of rock as a force of rebellion. Has rock's subversive quality been subverted by its increasingly close relationship with corporate America? If so, Jagger would be as much to blame as anyone. The Rolling Stones were the first band to arrange a corporate endorsement for one of their tours, and Stones songs have been sold for advertising jingles, most notably "Start Me Up" for a Macintosh computer TV spot.

"I don't think rock's power has been subverted, but I don't think sponsorship is such a wonderful thing. I try to restrict the use of Stones songs for ads; I don't control the publishing rights for all the songs, but the ones I do control, I never give to ads. I think it dilutes the music, because then you tend to think of a beer or a soft drink every time you hear it. But we're not living in East Germany pre-1989 here. People want to make a buck and they'll make it any way they can. That's why rap groups can't wait to get asked to do ads, and they'll do them."

So after all the years, all the sales of records and T-shirts and now computers, does Jagger still feel, when he sits down at a piano, that music has the power to move him? Can it still make his blood rise, or has he seen behind the facade for so long that rock and roll has lost its drama?

"Rock and roll can really move you emotionally, but I don't think you can compare rock as a work of art to a painting by Raphael or a great poem by Keats or Baudelaire. Yet rock does have a great visceral power. That's the power of music, it's very emotional. I don't think rock has the depth of those other things, but it's not supposed to.

"I think young people can still get out of rock exactly the same thing you could get out of it twenty-five years ago. I think older people have a mixed reaction to seeing us. I'm sure part of the experience is just reliving their youth for the day. Of course I just do it for the day too. I don't live it."

Despite all the fame and all the ways Jagger has changed over the years, he hasn't changed the way he relates to audiences. "When I'm playing at a club now, I feel exactly the same as when I was young. It all depends on the place, on the eruption that's going on."

A few days after the show in D.C., I saw the Stones again at the Meadowlands in New Jersey. Again, the Stones opened with a raw cover of the Buddy Holly tune "Not Fade Away," and it was clear that after a few days on the road the lava in the Stones' rhythm section had warmed considerably. Maybe the band just felt more relaxed or had remembered that they had nothing to prove. Jagger was sublime, voice booming, bounding the stage with sly, reptilian energy remarkable for a fifty-one-year-old man.

The glory of the Stones' live show had returned once again to its enduring secret: imprecision. Sparks fly and you're not at all sure where they'll fall. "Satisfaction" erupted, and Keith Richards's guitar sounded like his fuzz box might be broken, a searing, wiry sound that discomfited the normal ear. Sixty thousand people were on their feet with Jagger, chanting "I CAN'T GET NO SATISFAC-TION," arguably the anthem phrase of the postwar era. Jagger seemed as if he were laughing the words out, his vocalizing a slurred caricature of itself. Richards played a three-note solo that chipped away at the beat in corrosive polyrhythm.

Some music critics seem stuck on the fact that Mick Jagger is older than the current president of the United States. They ask what it means that these degenerates have failed to shrivel up, crawl off, and die. They would do well to think of other elders who reveled in nastiness and eternal adolescence, from Jean Genet to Pablo Picasso to Muddy Waters, from whose song the Rolling Stones took their name.

Although Jagger seems in some ways like a mere technocrat, it is only because the contribution he's made to pop culture is so ingrained in our imagination that we hardly notice it anymore. The wonder is that he has managed to remain imaginative for so long. It's one thing to create a single masterpiece, but it's quite another to continue writing and recording for more than thirty years without a break. One factor that's kept the songwriting process fresh for Jagger is that when the creative rush comes upon him, it comes as a surprise. It is a delicate state of mind to enter and cannot be forced.

"When you're creating something—before the craft element sets in—you get into this state of mind where you let all sorts of things bubble up. No matter how deep they may have been, they bubble up and come out. That's the feeling I get: they rise to the surface if you give them the right atmosphere to come out. Whatever atmosphere it is, whether it's the back of a taxi or a beautiful field in the country, it can be conducive to things bubbling up.

"It's very pleasing when that is happening. I feel

like it's not really me, it's something that I'm just a conduit for. I don't feel, 'Wow! I'm incredible! Look at what I just did.' I am pleased with myself at the end of it all—and why shouldn't you be?—but while I'm actually doing it, it's like, 'Where did that come from? I'm so glad I got that!' And 'I'm very pleased I got this bit—where'd it come from, that's strange!' But that's the typical creative process, isn't it? Now, whether this is good for your ego is another thing, but it certainly feels that you're just part of the process."

Having been the subject of so much criticism and acclaim over three decades, has Jagger become happier and more at ease with himself as a human being? "It's difficult to measure. I'm much more patient and relaxed, but that just comes from being more mature, and I think that when you're young and raw and brash, you want to establish your ego and stamp everything with it. Then when you've had some acclaim, you don't feel the need to do that as much. But I will continue to stamp everything, I mean, I'm not going to stop."

MEREDITH MONK

In Search of the Primal Voice

MEREDITH MON

In a spacious fifth-floor walk-up in lower Manhattan, six men and five women are arranged in a semicircle. Facing them, the composer and choreographer Meredith Monk conducts their voices in swells, her small body undulating like a reed of grass. The room, which serves as Monk's living and working space, is filled with harmony, vocal and otherwise. A rehearsal manager follows the proceedings, making notations on sheet music, and a pianist accompanies on an ancient electronic keyboard.

Monk, who is one of America's best-known and most adventurous avant-garde artists, is running her troupe through the paces of *Dawn*, a nonsectarian service to be presented at the Union Theological Seminary in New York. An air of informality suffuses the proceedings despite the sense of sacredness her music imparts. Photos of the Dalai Lama are the only noticeable decorations, except for a giant white papier-mâché turtle discreetly mounted on one of the far walls, which are also painted white. Monk's keyboard player, a slender man in his forties, brings an error in the sheet music to her attention. A subtle discussion follows, concerning the manner in which a single note is to be held and articulated, and whether a vowel could be pronounced more organically.

Monk is wearing ornately embroidered Chinese slippers, baggy black sweatpants, and a shockingly fuchsia

shirt that matches her socks. She commands eleven dis-
creet voices as though they were one living pipe organ.
The music feels vaguely Gregorian. As she speaks, she occasionally punctuates her talk with body language, short
little dance movements that wordlessly express the joy her
work gives her.

Monk talks about sound as though it were architectural, directing her singers to envision vocal crescendos
crashing through walls of long, solid notes. The chorus
weaves a nectarlike squall, at once sharp and soothing. It
has an enveloping effect: nothing breaks the trance until
Monk stops suddenly to question why no one is singing a
certain part. Soon the rehearsal begins again. The floor-
boards vibrate slightly as the chorus builds with waves of
long, open notes and counterpoints of sharp, fluttering
phrases. The singers are also dancers, of course, so they're
dressed in sweatpants and slippers, but at the moment they
are seated, fine-tuning their breathing, working hard to
develop clarity in the way their voices move together.
Monk asks them to explore the rhythm of a single note.
The work is painstaking and often microscopically detailed, like fixing individual stitches in a quilt.

I first met Monk on a bright Saturday morning, a
day after the rehearsal. It was the first spring day in New
York, a morning of such shimmery pleasure that to step
indoors for even an hour required a lot of willpower. Near
the buzzer, the words *Meredith Monk* were written in black
magic marker on a chipped piece of wood, so that only a
few of the letters were visible. Because Monk's building
lacks the requisite electrical system to buzz visitors in, she
dropped a small red silk purse down from her fifth-floor
window. It landed on a sunny patch of sidewalk with a
nearly inaudible thump. Inside was the key to the front
door.

There is something almost anachronistic about the ultradiminutive Monk. Perhaps it is the ease with which she inhabits her tiny body, the rightness of the way she moves, but she seems like a traveler from a past time when people were simply shorter, and it is the rest of us who are grotesquely tall by comparison. At fifty-two years old, she is probably the most well-preserved human being I have ever met—save for those who sleep in formaldehyde. She easily looks fifteen years younger.

Her work, which for more than thirty years has combined experimental music and movement in a series of award-winning films, albums, and live performances, has always been concerned with the potential of art to break down habitual patterns. "A habit really keeps you from being in the now," she says. "It's not that a pattern is good or bad, but I'm concerned with trying to be as much as possible in the moment. Habitual patterns are problematic only insofar as the pattern is not conscious.

"Structurally, I'm interested in forms that are not linear. In our culture the concept of narrative is something that people expect in theater, and in music they expect a certain kind of development, meaning they expect things to build, have a peak, and resolve in some way. I'm interested in creating work that is much closer to the way the mind works, which is definitely not a linear set of patterns. My forms are more circular or 'spiralic'—they don't really develop in a line and go to a climax, and then to a denouement. I work organically with the voice, and so in a sense my music is much more primal. I'm really trying to get to a more essential sense of music."

This search for the essence of the music requires Monk to find the most direct path to make any given musical statement. And what she has discovered is that finding the essence often means doing less rather than more, thereby allowing the power of the music to exist in the listener's imagination. "Composing is about leaving a lot of space, so that an audience can feel themselves in a very strong way, as well as the experience they're having. When the audience sees performers trying to manipulate, it is not satisfying. What I try to do is create forms that do not have that manipulative aspect. It's like trying to get down to the thing itself. That means leaving a lot of space for the audience to experience a performance in a very individual way. The pieces that feel like they have that sense of truth, that 'essence,' are the ones that feel like they've made themselves. So the process is getting out of the way of something that already exists, something that has its own laws and its own world."

If the great art already exists and the job of an artist is simply to be the conduit, how does Monk balance the requirements of discipline with the moment of inspiration? "Well, there *is* a discipline to it," she says with a knowing smile. "You have to be a good craftsman. You're lucky when that inspiration comes, but the other times you still practice your craft.

"In a sense, the joy is the daily work. Working every day is a little like coming back to the breath when you're practicing meditation. Any thoughts can come up but you're always coming back to the fundamental breath. Simply working every day has that same aspect to it, and that's also what keeps every day different." Whether she's composing music or meditating, by developing precise, present-minded awareness of the smallest changes that constantly take place, Monk is able to remain interested in the craftsmanship.

Monk first came across Buddhism as a student, but it was in the summer of 1975, when she went to the Naropa Institute in Boulder, Colorado, to teach some workshops, that she encountered the Shambala tradition established by the Tibetan Buddhist teacher Chögyam Trungpa, which would have such a major impact on her life and work. "It was at Naropa that I first realized how close what I had intuitively been doing in my work was to the principles of Buddhist practice. I noticed a great sense of space and quiet in the audiences I encountered at Naropa, which was something I was always working on. Then I heard some of Trungpa's talks, and those were just wonderful: I was able to see a strong link between my little path and the Shambala tradition. Still, I had some fears about organized religion, and I was a little wary about what might appear from the outside to be a cult or something."

Monk returned as a teacher to Naropa, circling around Buddhism, meeting Buddhist teachers. As the seventies drew to a close, events in her personal life came to a standstill, and a formal Buddhist practice seemed like a way to alleviate some of the stress. "I was entangled in some personal situations and needed to get some space into those situations. Then I read *Shambhala: The Sacred Path of the Warrior*. The Shambala path really felt right, and when I finally began the practice, I almost felt tears of relief.

"My whole way of seeing life has changed completely from doing the Shambala practice. Ten years ago, because performing came easy to me, I was very impatient with other people; I had what I call the ballet-master mentality, which is based on the illusion that by scaring people they'll do better. Because of doing this practice, I've learned to be much more compassionate about people's vulnerabilities as performers and workers, and as human beings, and as a performer myself, I've become a lot more vulnerable, a lot more comfortable with physical vulnerability and not knowing what's going to happen next."

Monk says that one of the reasons her pieces are always changing is her sense of art as an organic process. It's why she prefers live performance to film or recording: the impermanence and mutability of the form are paramount. Monk's work reflects a total commitment to kinesthetic organicity—to doing what comes naturally and spontaneously to the human body. Ultimately, all of her creations are about human connection, about people needing one another and rejoicing in the discovery of their interconnectedness.

Although Monk's performances require tremendous discipline and skill, they are more concerned with ideas than with technique. One of the major themes of her musical compositions is what one writer called "the archeology of the voice," reflecting Monk's fascination with the basic human utterance. For Monk, the voice is a language in itself. It has landscapes, states of being, personae, characters, textures, and psychic states.

"When you use the voice as an instrument, without necessarily using lyrics, you come across emotions that we don't have words for, very subtle shades of feeling that we can't articulate. When you dig down into the voice, you come across something like the memories of the human race. By working with the instrument of the voice in all of its possibilities, you also come across sounds that exist in other cultures. For me it's comforting, because I feel like part of the world vocal family."

Monk's compositions are often deceptively basic, as though we should somehow already know them. In *Facing North*, which she created with Robert Een in 1992, two people peep notes at each other in a volley known as hocketing, a medieval European technique in which a melody is composed by a pair of singers "throwing notes at each other through space," as Monk describes it. "It really is meditative, because you have to be right on the dot, all the time." Created while she was in Banff, Alberta, *Facing North* exemplifies the way Monk draws inspiration from physical landscapes and atmosphere. "I was so inspired by being there with the snow coming down. I was very interested in creating a duet form that's not about codependency, but about interdependency. *Facing North* was basically about the tenderness and fortitude of two people surviving in a barren, snowy landscape."

Monk has always held that creating art could be about far more than entertainment. "I think that art has the potential to be a healing force in society. In many cultures it is closely aligned with spiritual practices, and doing it can be transformational. So I spend a lot of time thinking about how art can be functional. Short of going into a monastery, I believe that creating art is one of the most spiritual things a person can do."

MOBY

Jesus Raves

If you've ever seen any of the nature documentaries on public television that explore animal life on the Serengeti Plains of Africa, you may recall the image of a pride of lions silhouetted against the horizon. Like a miniature, living diorama of those fierce but motionless animals, a family of cockroaches stands atop a clock in the one-bedroom apartment where Richard Melville Hall lives on the Lower East Side of Manhattan. Hall, whose stage name is Moby, is one of the best-known makers of ambient dance music (and a distant relative of *Moby Dick* author Herman Melville's). He lives in peaceful coexistence with the roaches because his values as a Christian prevent him from killing any living beings. He says that he likes to think of the insects in the same way other people look at lions on PBS documentaries, with a kind of benevolent admiration for their dignity. With the detached curiosity characteristic of the thirty-one-year-old musician, he hypothesizes that the roaches are drawn to the top of the clock by the slight warmth of its electric motor, or perhaps soothed by its vibrations. There is something willfully contrarian about Moby, a delight he takes in defying expectations.

His iconoclastic lifestyle defies our assumptions about born-again Christians, and his music, while often devotional, is light-years from the dogmatic and saccharine literalism of contemporary Christian music. Moby has done dance remixes for Michael Jackson, Depeche Mode, the B-52's, and most recently, Metallica, but although he is best known for his early association with ambient house, techno, and rave culture, his style is decidedly eclectic and definitely not ideal for drifting off into a trance. His most recent work is defined by a return to his punk rock roots and sheer sonic aggression, however un-Christian that might seem.

"I think aggression's a really important part of who I am," he says, "and I really like that side of me. I like that side of a lot of people. But there are appropriate and inappropriate expressions of aggression. I draw the line at physically imposing your will on another person or creature. Anything I do to myself or another consenting adult is fine, but the moment I force my will on another creature, that's when it becomes ethically suspect."

The title of Moby's major-label debut, *Everything Is Wrong*, makes obvious his frustrations with the direction of the world, which are detailed in liner notes on environmental problems, animal testing, and other issues. One of the songs is a howling industrial track called "All I Need Is to Be Loved," in which he repeats the title phrase over and over, accompanied by a frantic, gnashing beat. "That song was a visceral expression of desperation," he says. "I didn't know what sort of love I wanted—whether love of a friend, love of a mate, or God's love." Indeed, one of the major factors in his decision to devote his life to music is this need for love and connection.

"I find making music is a great way to connect with others, on a very selfish level. As far as the humanitarian aspect, I'm striving to be honest as a public figure and as a musician, because I think that one way of ameliorating suffering is through honesty. Not pushing suffering aside, but expressing it in an honest way, saying, 'This is who I

understand myself to be. I might be flawed, but I'm not trying to present myself as perfect.'

"One thing I think is dangerous in a lot of religious cosmologies is that they set up a paradigm of what the right way to be is. So when people get involved with religious discipline, they say, 'Well, I don't look, sound, or think like the Dalai Lama, so I must be a failure.' There are these weird paradigms, especially when Westerners interpret Eastern religions. When I was in high school, I tried to be a Taoist, and I felt like a failure because I didn't think like Alan Watts. You know, here's this smart guy living in California who understands the secrets of the universe, and I get it on an intellectual level but it doesn't resonate within me, so I must be inadequate. On the other hand, there's also a danger in people successfully emulating some paradigm and thinking there's enlightenment in that."

In the last five years, Moby has moved away from emulating the paradigm of the good Christian. In the late 1980s, when I first met him, he was celibate and abstained from alcohol and drugs. "I was trying to be a good, meek, mild-mannered Christian. I was emulating the Christian paradigm that was instilled in me as a child. The weird thing is, there isn't much precedent for it in the character of Christ, because Christ was extremely dynamic: he swore, and he drank, and he ran around, and he screamed at people. He loved his friends and was a very human, passionate figure. So I rejected that weird asceticism after thinking about who Christ really was and realizing that I was forcing myself to be something that didn't feel natural."

Years after his frustrating high-school encounter with the writings of Alan Watts, one of the things that occupies his thoughts now is the notion of "flow," which would appear to be a Taoist precept, although Moby is reluctant to label it as such. "There might be a lot of truth in Taoism, but I wonder why we need to call it something. Instead of 'Buddha,' why can't we call it 'Coke can'? People get caught up in thinking that using a certain word or wearing a certain article of clothing makes you more enlightened.

"It's really hard to approach this stuff without baggage, and as a Christian I deal with that all the time. I don't even like to say 'Christ' or 'Christian,' because those words mean one thing to me and something different to everyone else. Once I was signing autographs at a rock festival in Detroit and someone came up to me and said, 'I think it's really cool that you're a Christian.' And the guy standing next to her said, 'You're a Christian? That's fucked up,' and walked away. They were both responding to that word *Christian*, and I wanted to say to them, 'Look, I like both of you, but neither one of you probably understands what that word means.' "

Fascinated by ethical questions, Moby seems to have a constitutional aversion to taking things at face value. He constantly wonders about the original sources of social and psychological conventions, and about what might be called the ancestral motives of the human psyche. "When I get very jealous, for example, what am I really expressing? There's the simplistic understanding, 'I'm jealous because I'm in love with this person,' but really it's much deeper than that. You can look at it from the evolutionary perspective, which is that jealousy is a survival function: if you have a community and you have a mate, your chances of surviving and passing on your DNA are a lot stronger. It's something that's inbred in us.

"One of the goals in my life is striving toward increasing awareness, through whatever means possible. That's why I like to make tests of strange behavior, like

going out and getting really, really drunk, or having inappropriate one-night stands. My experience is that there's
wisdom in things that might seem really delusional, because they foster humility. I used to look at alcoholics and
judge them really harshly, thinking alcoholism was a weakness. Before I took mushrooms about a year ago I was
really judgmental about drugs. I have this moral superiority problem: if you're doing something I think is wrong
and I'm not, there's a part of me that feels superior.

"So humility is a good thing, but there are some
things that shouldn't be tolerated. One is using animals for
human purposes, because that creates so much suffering.
Sure, my righteous superiority complex is tied up in this,
but I've moved to a level on the issue of animal rights that
most people haven't got to. When you get there, you realize how terrible the situation is.

"I'm a big believer in utilitarian expediency. If I
want people to stop eating meat, I've got to deal with them
the way I'd like to be dealt with, and I think people are
more responsive to compassion. The problem is I get exas-
perated with how horrible human culture is, what a waste
of time most human activity is. We have for so long squan-
dered our potential. I actually place a little more value on
animal suffering than I do on human suffering, because
I'm not a big fan of human beings. I don't dislike humans;
it's the love-hate thing, you know: the more you love somebody, the more they hurt you. I expect so much from myself and from humanity, and humanity often disappoints
me, and I always disappoint myself."

Perhaps Moby's anger and disappointment with humanity is the flip side of his need for love. Tormented by
apocalyptic visions of where society is headed, he longs for
a just and compassionate world where everyone loves
everyone else. In the meantime, he says, he'd also like to

get some love for himself. "I have this primal need, and on one level I take it pretty seriously, as we all do. On another level, I recognize that I'm one of five billion people, one out of a trillion creatures on this planet, and my subjective experience is really inconsequential. When I sing 'All that I need is to be loved,' I recognize intellectually that 'I' is kind of a spurious construct, yet I take that 'I' really seriously. Pop music constantly glorifies the 'I.' The deified musician is saying 'I take myself very seriously,' and that justifies the listeners' taking themselves seriously, and it creates this weird emphasis on subjective experience.

"When I first got involved with dance music culture in the late 1980s, there was something transcendent about it. I grew up listening to very self-serious music, like Joy Division, where the self is very well constructed. Then along came hip-hop, where the 'I' was like a parody or a caricature of the 'I' in rock music. Then you get to disco and dance music, where the 'I' meant 'we,' because you're part of a mass of people dancing, and when a woman is singing, 'I love you,' everyone is singing it. There was something really nice about that. Now that celebratory 'I/we' has increasingly been rejected by dance culture and I'm returning to the 'I' of Joy Division, which resonates with me in a deeper, more distilled way than when I was an adolescent. When I was fifteen, I hadn't experienced all that much. Now I'm thirty, twice as old, and the loneliness has gotten a lot deeper. I feel that desperation, the need to be loved and connect with other people. Now my life is a lot more desolate.

"On an ordinary day, I'll wake up, go to work, and suddenly eight o'clock in the evening rolls around and I won't have spoken face-to-face with another human being all day. Then a friend will come over and I won't know how to talk to him. It's kind of upsetting to realize that people you're close to are not guitar amplifiers you can do whatever you want with. You actually have to interact with them. When I'm making music, I do think about other people a lot, but it's sort of an automatic process. I will be thinking about the structure of the music I'm working on, but at the same time I'm thinking, how will this resonate with other people? Am I providing a service for other people? Will it make them like me more?"

Moby was born in New York City in 1965. His father died when he was two, and he moved up to Connecticut with his mother, whom he describes as "a sort of broke secretary-painter-hippie. And her boyfriends were, like, rock musicians and gas station attendants. We were living with my grandparents, who were wealthy, WASP types, so it was really weird, because all my friends came from stable nuclear families and I had this mother who was sleeping with the guy who pumped the gas in their Jaguars."

Moby dropped out of college after stints at the University of Connecticut and the State University of New York in Purchase, majoring in philosophy and English, and devoted himself to music full-time. He had played guitar since the age of ten, including a high school stint with the seminal punk act the Vatican Commandos, who released a seven-inch single ("Hit Squad for God," backed with "Wonderbread") that is still a collectible among hardcore punk enthusiasts. At the time he began deejaying, Moby was an atheist suburban punk, but around the age of twenty he had an epiphany. "I was talking about God one day with a friend of mine who was a youth minister, and he realized that even though I had been brought up ostensibly Christian, I didn't know anything about who Christ was. So he suggested that I read the New Testament. This was around 1985. I read about five minutes of Matthew and that was it. It was like talking to someone for five minutes and realizing that you're in love with them and you want to spend the rest of your life with them. I became a Christian and a vegan, and as a deejay, I became interested in dance music, whereas three years before that, I hated dance music, made fun of my vegetarian friends, and was a militant atheist."

Moby doesn't go to church, although for a while after his conversion, he attempted to make it a habit. "There's this ascetic paradigm of what a Christian should be and I tried to adhere to it for a while. But it was more about the institution than about me as an individual, and a central theme of Christianity is that institutions should serve the individual, not vice versa. I was trying to be a good lawful Christian, but it didn't work. I had to reevaluate my beliefs and discern what was baggage and what was true for me."

Moby was living in a loft in a converted factory in Stamford at this time and making a living as a deejay. He began building a small studio and started venturing into Manhattan to solicit record companies. After numerous rejections, he met people who were starting a new label called Instinct Records. Instinct signed him for zero dollars in 1990 and began releasing his singles. One of them, "Go," became a hit in Europe, selling nearly half a million copies.

By 1991 Moby was unhappy with his deal with Instinct, and he spent a year in a lawsuit trying to get out of his contract. Eventually he signed with Elektra Records, who released the *Move* EP in 1993 and then his first full-length album, *Everything Is Wrong*, in 1994. His third album, *Animal Rights*, was released in 1996.

"My music is either a utopian thing—trying to see the world as beautiful and wonderful—or dystopian. In either case, I'm setting up these exaggerated, romantic versions of what bliss and dystopia are like. The new album is almost all dystopic—it's either adolescent lonely rage or a sort of resigned sadness. I'm into blunt, monolithic expression, which, if you scratch the surface, has ambiguity.

"It's a very intuitive approach to decreasing people's suffering. It's nice to feel like there's someone out there you can connect with, who makes you feel like your loneliness is somehow more than mundane. That's a big job that art has—to make the ordinary crap of our lives seem noble. There are so many institutions in our culture that lead people down the path of delusion that I think making music that people can connect to is a defensible service to provide. If I made music that was all bliss and joy, that wouldn't be honest, that would be conforming to a paradigm, like I tried to do with Christianity.

"So I rebel against that dishonesty. When I was a punk rocker, I tried to force myself to be a good punk rocker. And when I was a fledgling Christian, I tried to force myself to be a good fledgling Christian—based on my twisted ideas of what these paradigms were. Now I realize I'm just this weird little animated mass of material that has a character I have to be true to. It's so easy to dismiss something when it looks the way you expect. That's why I love surrealism, and why I loved being a punk rocker fifteen years ago, because you take something conventional and twist it. What's more interesting? A lama who wears a saffron robe and has his head shaved like a million others, or a lama who lives in a flophouse in New York City and is an alcoholic? As far as I'm concerned, enlightenment can be had when you're drunk out of your mind on a subway at four in the morning with your teeth missing because you've just had the shit kicked out of you. Every moment of our lives is potentially laden with meaning. Humility, observation, and striving for awareness is all we need to do."

IGGY POP

Once in a While, When White People Loosen Up

In a small café on Avenue B and Tenth Street, in what used to be a scary neighborhood before New York City policemen in riot gear drove out the squatters, homeless, sickos, and wanna-be sickos who lived in Tompkins Square Park and the abandoned hulls of Alphabet City, on a corner now as fully gentrified as a mall, I sit face-to-face with the Ig.

He lives in the neighborhood and, to his credit, moved here before it was the fancy-pants thing to do. Of course, back then he couldn't have afforded a fashionable neighborhood: although the name Iggy Pop and the Stooges has been in the rock lexicon for a quarter century, he only started making a real living a few years ago. Anyway, there's little chance that anyone would confuse him with a bourgeois college kid, slumming it for kicks. A glance at his face will tell you why.

Sitting just inches away from that face and sipping tea with Iggy is a vivid experience. The skin is sucked tight against his skull, as though someone had attached a powerful vacuum to the back of his head and pulled all the meat up against the underlying bone structure. He has big, bulging, blue marbles for eyes and his hands look like they belong on a dead man. He has a habit of lurching forward and leering for emphasis, which, coupled with the fact that his features look like those of a man encountering severe G-force, creates a sort of night-of-the-living-dead-jack-in-the-box effect.

Impish, campy, and gleefully degenerate, Iggy has long been both mascot and avatar of the punk rock scene. He was nearly one of its martyrs, too, having by his own recollection injected, smoked, inhaled, and eaten fourteen illegal drugs. All of this has until recently kept him safely outside of mainstream popular culture, but in the last year two films have prominently featured his music: *Trainspotting* and *Basquiat*, both of which have a heroin connection. The opening sequence of *Trainspotting* is accompanied by the title track of *Lust For Life*, a 1977 Iggy Pop album produced by David Bowie (which was the real-life sound track of choice among British heroin addicts at that time). Another one of Iggy's songs, "Search and Destroy," was used in a recent commercial for Nike. It seems the people who were once ashamed to admit they were Iggy Pop fans have grown up to run film studios and ad agencies.

Even Hollywood seems to have discovered the value of his weathered looks. He recently finished filming a starring role in his first big-budget movie, *The Crow II*— although he may be in danger of being typecast: he describes the role as "enforcer for a drug boss, addicted to motorcycles, drugs, and killing insects." "Iggy is the icon of the degenerate rock and roll lifestyle," says Jim Jarmusch, who directed him in the 1995 art-house film *Dead Man*. "He's like the Bruce Lee of rock and roll. But he survived."

As a musician, Iggy Pop (real name James Osterburg) ranks among rock's most physical performers. He has slashed himself onstage, rolled around bare-chested on broken glass, and picked fights with audience members. After spending time in a mental institution in the seventies,

Iggy says he endured most of the eighties "in somebody else's car, in possession of something illegal, on my way from something illegal to something illegal, with many illegal things happening all around me."

In view of all this self-destructive activity, it is not surprising that when he looks back on his life, the word *anger* pops up a lot. Anger as artistic inspiration. Anger as career motivation. Anger as modus operandi. Anger as drug. Anger as anger. When I asked him if he knew what the anger was all about, he made a frightening gesture, as though under different circumstances he might have simply started banging my head against the floor, and said, "Now you're getting a little too close to what your parents do." (Both my parents are clinical psychologists.) All he would say about the childhood roots of his rage—and he kept saying it over and over like a mantra—was: "I just wasn't very happy. I was not very happy. I was not a happy person."

His early performances were extremely confrontational. Pop describes the vibe during the first twenty years of his career as a professional performer as "often very, very tense and very much an adversarial relationship. Stuff just happened. It depended very much on audience interaction—on what mood I was in and the people around me and how we interacted. There might be some cops I didn't like and there would be a problem with them. If you see film from when I started out in my early twenties, it's pretty hilarious, because it appears that this guy is so stoned he's really not capable of any major energy for more than ten seconds at a time. You'll see this guy lurching and swaying and all of a sudden: '*Blaalalalala!*' for a few seconds, a burst of craziness, usually directed at somebody, reaching out to grab somebody or throw himself at something. I just didn't think about it. I'd go out there and I'd have this music and this certain way I was going to sing it, and after the show it would be like, 'What the fuck happened? Boy, that was some night.'

"Ultimately, my way of performing can't be reduced to a list of shocking things I did onstage. It's the vibe and the quality of the thing; it's about totally losing yourself and understanding that what you're doing right here, right now, is the most important thing in the world."

During his concerts over the years he has urinated, defecated, vomited, spit, brawled, ranted, raved, wept, and, in his own words, "performed every human bodily function known to man." Once, when I saw him perform, he stuck his finger up his ass and then popped it in his mouth. But to get stuck in shock or disgust would miss the point. There are lessons to be learned from his wildness—the raging shock tactics were symbols of Pop's total bravery and surrender. He didn't set out to shock people just for the sake of it, or to hide meager musical talent, or to get rich and famous. He did shocking things because he was devoted to performing with 100 percent of himself; he surrendered all self-control to connect fully with the music. That required a degree of self-sacrifice and commitment rare in the arts: he was searching so wildly and fully for an experience free of bullshit that he was willing to die for it.

"When we played—and this was a good sign—the outline of heads at the back of the room would freeze in position for the entire gig. Nobody moved. Nobody moved because they were interested. Nobody went to the bathroom, nobody bought a drink, nobody went to pick up a girl. They just stood there and watched. We stopped everybody. People are looking for something: sometimes it's delivered, but more often I find that performers are just an enormous amount of hot air and the audiences let them get away with it.

"It's obvious that rock and roll is a religion; it's formatted exactly as a religion. You're out there in the audience, and you see a person or a group of people take the stage, and those first moments of music are really powerful. The music cascades off you like crystals, like little crystals of energy, and those people onstage are transformed. They're living gods at that moment—you're looking at humans made gods. That fascinates people because their day-to-day existence, which is so tawdry, doesn't measure up to it.

"I've had spiritual experiences at rock concerts. I was about fourteen years old the first time I saw Jerry Lee Lewis. It was at a barn dance out near Ann Arbor, and I had a spiritual experience when he stepped up on the stage, sneering. I was shocked at how pasty and white his face was. It was white like a ghost, and his hair was so intensely peroxided that it reflected all the light from the spotlights. White rays of light were bouncing off his head. I'd never been baptized, but it was like Catholicism when it works. It was like, *Ahhhhhhhhhh*! I wanted to be him. He got up there and he sneered. They gave him a piano to play and he looked at it once, made a sneer, kicked it, and said, 'I ain't playin' that,' and walked off. He finally deigned to come back on, and he sneered and mimed a country song and split. But I had a practically religious experience, you know. I liked the way that light bounced off his peroxided hair and I liked the way his complexion looked, like it was out of the grave. It gave me a signal, something about that artificiality. I thought, WOW, this person's obviously in another world, and that turned me on."

Iggy grew up in Ann Arbor, Michigan, in a racially charged era when the nearest city, Detroit, was transformed into a ghost town of burned-out buildings by race riots in the summer of 1967. His music can be understood as a reaction to the white power structure by a guy who was too cool to be down with the race that invented the bunny hop. Iggy and his pals were the meanest and weirdest of the superfreaks and delinquents who populated suburban America in the late 1960s. Their stance was a total "fuck you" to conventional thinking, even to the prevailing feel-good hippie revolution. Like the Velvet Underground, who had just finished touring America as part of Andy Warhol's Plastic Exploding Inevitable, Iggy was punk almost a decade before Malcolm McLaren invented the Sex Pistols.

"I found America very brutal in junior high and high school. You had to fight all the time. In my school, the high point of the day would be to see one of the school bullies push some other guy until he would react, then everybody would go to watch the fight. I never won. I almost killed a guy once because he was just beating me so bad. I was fighting a black guy, and he just kept doing my face until I finally grabbed him by the neck and started beating his head on the gymnasium floor. And I thought at that time, I could kill this person. Some guy pulled me off; I think it was the gym coach. I was not happy about that.

"I wasn't a happy kid and somewhere along the line, I started hanging out with juvenile delinquents and that became the Stooges."

The little-known event to which the beginnings of punk can be traced was rather mundane—his manager turned off the heat in the studio where Iggy and the Stooges rehearsed. The big bang that gave birth to punk took place in 1968, while the Stooges were running through the same old chords, searching for their sound and trying not to give up hope.

"The Stooges had been practicing for a year, and our manager said, 'That does it, I'm fed up,' and he turned off the heat in our rehearsal room. And what happened was that I got so angry that suddenly I was in the music. I started dancing around, jumping up and down, and screaming at him. I was running around with my mike and insulting him and I looked at the musicians, and I saw a reaction—suddenly they weren't playing the same. They were impressed. Obviously I wacked 'em, I touched them, I got to them. I was on something, I think it was either DMT or some other kind of psychedelic. It was a very cold day, there was snow outside, and I was determined to make it. It took a while to get things together. It was a combination of my determination, anger, and the drugs, and a really good beat. We had started out as a band playing very quiet and nonviolent songs, but after a while I realized that ain't gonna cut it. People want some juice. So, I said, 'Okay, you want some juice? I'll give you some juice.' "

It was around this time that Pop began spending time with John Sinclair, legendary founder of the White Panther party. Sinclair, now a respected deejay living in New Orleans, had a close relationship with the seminal Detroit band the MC5. "I got hooked up with Sinclair and them because they were the coolest bunch of guys around town, and the ones that could access an audience for me. The White Panthers had a political platform that consisted of three things: rock and roll, dope, and fucking in the streets. And they printed it on postcards with a white panther, saying, 'Fucking in the streets! Tell your friends!' "

As kid brothers to the MC5, Iggy Pop and the Stooges were an integral part of Sinclair's world. "Sinclair had this thing called the Trans Love Commune, which meant that basically he could take all the money from the bands' gigs and have lots of girls and smoke lots of dope. But on the other hand, because of this guy, I was listening to John Coltrane and Archie Shepp and Miles Davis, while two hundred miles down the road in Chicago, you had the Buckinghams listening to Young Rascals records. Sinclair had a bigger vision than just trying to do songs that sounded like what was on the radio. No, it was: 'We're going to blow up America and then we're all going to metamorphose into black people with white skin, and we're gonna be fucking in the streets.' It was like, WOW, this guy's thinking big. And that started my egotism going: 'Oh, yeah? You think that's big? I'm gonna erase the universe! I'll one-up you, I'll be negative to everything.' "

Even today, when Pop talks about music, he still sounds a little bit like that wild-eyed, problack revolutionary. "Basically rock and roll was stolen. The idea of a kit of drums and people standing in front in this formation— bass to the left, guitar to the right, and the guy in front singing—was taken from small combo jazz and blues; the instrumentation was, certainly. That has segued into something white people know how to do, which is go to school and attend a lecture. Basically, a rock show is somebody giving a speech to people who are looking for and receiving guidance. Sometimes it transcends that and gets pretty sexy, and once in a while a white person gets loose and actually starts to move with the music.

"Heavy metal is the first kind of rock and roll that dropped the African influence in music. Heavy metal is white. There's no slip and slide to that. It's just crude, white, muscles bashing, and it has a lot of fascist overtones—and so there's all that going on, and that gets a huge reaction from the crowd."

"It used to be I got a lot of my energy from anger. My attitude was always, 'OK, I'll show you.' The best way to put it is, when you're out there on the stage, that's where you feel whether you're worth yourself or not."

This sense of underlying inadequacy, the feeling that he had something to prove, made for some combustible performances. "I think you're proving to yourself that you're alive, ultimately. I think that's the whole attraction. Originally the rock and roll format was for black music; white people waltzed, and before that they were listening to Beethoven, who was black anyway. But white people didn't really boogie. I think the wealth of this country and the degree of visible civilization that we've attained has made it tough for a white person to move. There's a lot to lose. But there's always a yearning inside, people trying to break loose in some way, to get out of that consciousness and change that consciousness."

Iggy attended the University of Michigan but dropped out after forming the Stooges. He managed to avoid the Vietnam War via a dramatic encounter with an army psychiatrist. ("I told them I wasn't the kind of person they wanted to draft. It took some acting.")

In the mid-1970s, Iggy spent a productive period in Berlin, along with sometime producer and collaborator David Bowie, who was also escaping the suicidal drug excesses of Los Angeles. "It was, I'm happy to say, totally un-American, which is why we could make good stuff there. What you had there was a sturdy, large city, a metropolis of a certain vintage that had been built to accommodate millions of people, in slightly damaged condition and holding only about seven hundred thousand residents. Everybody else had died or got thrown out or didn't want to live there because there was no economy. Berlin was buried in the middle of East Germany, so it was gloriously free of people of common sense and ambition.

"Bowie and I were there; he was looking for a way

out, he was looking for a new person to be. He had a wife at the time who wanted to set him up in a mansion in Switzerland, but he didn't want that. He had just barely survived a few years in L.A., he couldn't really go back there. Basically L.A. was and is a place where you get your ass kissed in direct commensuration with your fame and fortune. And there's all sorts of ambitious and capable people whose intentions are less than artistic. Whereas in Berlin, do you think a record company talent scout is gonna say, 'Yeah, I'll just stop off to see you in Berlin on my way to Prague'? You couldn't even go to Prague at that time."

"There were many Berlins: there was a Berlin that was this mysterious old falling-down city; then there were the modern edifices that they built to house people that the government was trying to encourage to live there. There were a lot of strange, lost kids and the whole 'Christiane F' scene, and lots of strange discos. But everything about that town had a wonderfully sinister vibe to it."

Iggy's mission in Berlin wasn't so much a matter of going to a foreign city to record an album as it was living in a foreign city as a form of indirect artistic inspiration—the idea was to go out there and have some experiences that might be good fodder for songwriting. The actual schedule of writing and recording was peripheral. "We would wake up in the late morning and very seldom go into the studio. We would try to have some sort of different activities. Because really, there are only certain periods when you want to sit down and try to write songs. In fact, the best way to kill your music is to sit down every day and work at it. You got to sneak up on it and catch it when it's not looking. So I'll go read a book or go see a picture or go hang out in a bar with some interesting people or go have an experience of some sort, feel something, and take in something new, get a new feeling, and then make some music. Make it real quick. When I'm at my best, I try to operate that way. I also work at it too. But you can never get too much that way."

Referring to the balance between inspiration and craftsmanship, Picasso once said something to the effect that genius doesn't happen very often, but when it struck, he was always standing right in front of the canvas. Iggy's credo in Berlin seemed to be, "Genius doesn't happen often, but it helps if you spend your time getting drunk with interesting people while you wait."

"The sort of work I was doing with Bowie in that period was not very craftsmanlike at all. It wasn't about practicing your guitar. For example, *Lust for Life* was written while we were watching TV: the armed forces network was on, and they had a mime of a telegraph signal that they used to announce the news show. It went, *Eeeeeee-eeeee-eeeeee-e-e-e-e*! Bowie heard that and picked up his son's toy, a plastic ukulele. He gave me the chords and I recorded it on a twenty-dollar mono tape recorder that I kept around for when he was in the mood. Then I put the words to it. To write the words, I'd take red wine and these little pills called Stern pills—they're pills that German kids take to study, they're like legal speed."

It was not until after Pop and Bowie had left Berlin and were living in Paris completing the recording of the *Lust For Life* album that Pop wrote what became one of his best-known songs, an ominous anthem to the demimonde of late seventies Berlin called "Night Clubbing." The tune, later covered by Grace Jones, perfectly encapsulates the sneering, perverse, and unhinged attitude of the time and place.

" 'Night Clubbing' was written fucking around, after we had finished recording 'The Idiot.' We were actually in France, but thinking German, and the sessions were all over, but I felt the album was incomplete. We were goofing around and the roadies were taking down the equipment, and they'd gotten two of those rubber masks of a hideous old scary person that mock age, age-mockery masks. And they put them on and went around the room, and Bowie's mask inspired him to sit at the piano and play what I would describe as kind of Hoagy Carmichael, old-man piano music. When I heard that piano music, I went, 'That's it! that's it, that's what I want.' I got very, very excited and forced him, just begged and pleaded with him, to record that. He said, 'But there's no band.' And I said, 'Let's just use this little drum machine.' He felt that it would be too cheap, because at the time nobody used shit like that.

"But the idea was basically to get the result; he wasn't thinking about it. If you try to do a good rock song, you can't do it. Or it's going to be very pedestrian. I mean, it might sell billions of copies, but it's still going to be pedestrian shit. Everybody's done some; he's done some before and so have I. The best things, you need to twist that somehow.

"One thing I found out is that what you usually set out to do isn't nearly as interesting as what actually happens. I guess to survive sometimes you gotta just relax and just watch and say, 'Okay, you like that? Okay, I'll go with that.' You never know what an audience is gonna react to."

In a sense, Berlin represented a new life for Bowie and Pop, who had both nearly gone over the abyss with drugs and drinking. "We had both been living that way in L.A., and in Berlin we'd slowed it way down. It would be more like every day just get up and try to do something normal and drink a couple of beers with lunch and then drink a little beer at dinner and just try to be like normal people. Once or twice a week, we would go out to a club and drink whisky and score some drugs and have a little bender, but we'd keep it within that limit. It wasn't the sort of thing where it's like, 'I've just scored half an ounce and I'm going to have a pile of this in my home for weeks.' We were on our way, both of us, away from that. Bowie was really haggard, he was really haggard."

Despite the considerably nonexemplary lifestyle he led, today Iggy has a wiry and muscular frame—so much so that even in a loose-fitting T-shirt his shoulders look like melons mounted on a skeleton. He does not lift weights or work out in any traditional way, and his diet is far from healthy. "I eat steaks, I like a lot of butter on my toast, I like a lot of eggs, and I fart constantly, all day."

Several years back Pop kicked his drug habit and began practicing chi kung, a system of Chinese exercises aimed at cultivating one's inner energy, or chi. Coincidentally or not, around this same time his music became more accessible, beginning with 1993's *American Caesar* and continuing with 1996's *Naughty Little Doggie*, and his career started becoming profitable. The violent confrontations cooled out. The audiences actually started smiling. The gigs were no longer a battle to the death. Perhaps his reservoirs of anger were simply tapped out, or he just got tired of all the drugs. Maybe something more poetic took place, a transformation or awakening of some kind. Either way, a watershed had been reached in his life as a performer.

But unlike a lot of reformed alcoholics or heavy drug users, Pop is not in the least bit preachy or ashamed. In fact, he believes that had it not been for the drugs he took, he might never have gotten to where he is today. "It's funny, because I'm a more sober person now and I've made sober moves which have allowed me to be rewarded, finally, for the things I did inebriated. Are drugs going to

change you that much as a person? No. If you take the
drugs, all it can do is destabilize certain parts of you. But if
you're a good artist, are drugs going to make your artistic
endeavors less impeccable? No. Are they going to make
them more inspired? No. Drugs can help you to stop paying attention to five hundred-thousand-and-three things
that you don't need to know about and just pay attention
to one thing that you want to know about. It can function
that way, especially with young people who still have a few
more brain cells left. But after you do it long enough, it's
like, how many times can you snap a bra? After a while, it
just won't snap back anymore. That's pretty much what
drugs are worth in my experience.

"These days, something really good happens when
I'm singing for people. It's not very esoteric or spiritual. I
just think I sang twenty-odd years and then, for some reason, the page turned. About three years ago, people
started smiling at me. People were beaming at me when I
sang, and as soon as they started beaming at me like that,
it changed everything."

The chi kung that Iggy began practicing when he
stopped taking drugs is a series of postures and movements executed in coordination with the breath. The goal
of chi kung is closely related to that of acupuncture: to increase the chi and stimulate its circulation through specific
pathways in the body, known in traditional Chinese medicine as meridians.

While embracing this admittedly esoteric practice,
Iggy is quick to downplay any mystical or spiritual overtones (despite the fact that chi kung does have a certain
meditative aspect). He emphasizes that his chi kung
teacher is, if not a brazen huckster, at least an ordinary guy
who digs chicks and cash and just happens to be able to
push his fingers through other people's bones, slowly.

"I'm a maniac about chi kung. I've been doing it for six or seven years and, basically, I've learned that I need it to survive. I study with a fellow named Don Ahn, he's my guide, my teacher. It's funny because everyone expects him to be a vegetarian and very holy, but he's not. He likes to get fucked and eat steaks, and he likes money—a lot. He's a guy, you know. He can also kill you in eight hundred ways, but he'd rather just take your money legally. He's like that.

"The chi kung has improved my confidence incredibly. I do it on a daily basis. When I have a problem, I think, 'Oh my God, this is terrible, I'm gonna fold.' Then I do some chi kung and I always feel better. It functions for me like meditation does for other people.

"As far as the energy stuff, I used to get that—in a bad way, I suppose—from the huge amplifiers and the drugs and the jolt you get from people's attention. I used to get out there and feel a real chi buzz."

Of course, what Iggy now refers to with hindsight as a chi buzz was probably a different kind of buzz, considering the fact that he was not practicing chi kung at the time and was gobbling lots of acid. "I used to be able to take multiple hits of strong LSD about a half hour before I went onstage, so just as I was starting to ying out, as that LSD was starting to shatter my psychic boundaries and expand me, I went out and did the gig. Then, *Shwooomf!* there'd be no expanding effect of the acid, I'd be totally focused. That energy from the LSD felt like somebody shoved a big electric stick right up my spine, and I'd kind of ride it like a horse. Then I'd get done with the gig and about twenty-five minutes later, *Booof!* the effects of the drug would come back. It would be like if you held a spring compressed between two hands for an hour at the gig, and then finally as I started to relax, *poooof!* The acid would say, 'Hi! I'm back, and you're really stoned! And you're not going to sleep tonight.'

"Eventually I got so I didn't need the drugs, all I needed was the loud amps and the drums. Because there's nothing like it, when you get out there and play for people. It may not be highly spiritually evolved or whatever—it's more about solving the basic things that are going on in my head. There was always something inside me that wanted to do music, to be in a band, to be a musician. I wanted to do it for my whole life. I always thought my talents were limited, but I thought, I'll do the best I can with what I've got and make sure never to do something hokey, and only do what I think is really good. I always believed that if I pleased myself, other people were going to follow me. They had to.

"But it didn't happen for a long time. I didn't start making a living until about ten years ago, and then it all came in at once. Before that, I had a little bit of my own money once in a while and other than that, I would live on the charity of other people. I never was in a band that made any money on a tour until I was about forty-five years old. The name Iggy Pop is big now, because I went out and worked like a dog and brought the material to people's attention. I just kept pushing it and pushing it and it finally happened. It's really very gratifying and also very strange, because it's made me a happy old man."

MICHAEL FRANTI

Discovering Rasta Roots by Way of New Zealand

There's no shortage of musicians willing to bitch about how the world has mistreated them. Rarer are artists who use their fifteen minutes of fame to focus on other people's suffering. Rarer still are straight songwriters, in any genre, who tackle the subject of gay-bashing. And when it comes to rap artists who champion gay rights, we're getting into the realm of extremely rare, as in, one. His name is Michael Franti.

A few years back, as a member of the Disposable Heroes of Hiphoprisy, Franti recorded "Language of Violence," the first anti-gay-bashing rap ever. In a realm as virulently intolerant and macho as rap—and just about everywhere else in American public discourse—defense of gay rights can be costly (remember the beating Bill Clinton took for supporting gays in the military). The track remains an oasis of sensitivity in a genre drenched in testosterone. The music is moody, nearly cinematic. The lyrics narrate a scene in which a young boy is humiliated at school, and ultimately fatally beaten, for being gay. In the end, his attacker is sent to jail, where he is raped by other inmates.

The thing that makes Franti stand out in the world of hip-hop isn't the depth but the breadth of his view: Franti took rap a step further than the usual danceable

complaints about the embattled condition of black America and focused on the dehumanizing qualities of bigotry outside the ghetto. In the context of the myopic tribalist concerns that can mar the music of any marginalized group, the point is not that Franti used rap as a vehicle to champion gay rights per se but that he dared to look beyond the suffering of black America.

His current group, Spearhead, continues to create socially conscious music that is at once Afrocentric and humanist. In recent years his lyrics have become more self-consciously "pro-black" (perhaps it became a credibility issue), but his attitude remains all-encompassing.

"As a person of color, I deal a lot with issues of race, and I've had to examine the similarities to the plight of the gay community. 'Language of Violence' could be about any number of incidents that I experienced growing up around a lot of teen angst and teen violence. Although the song is gay-specific, it's about a larger issue, which is male violence. I wanted to write a song specifically about antigay violence, but it's also about the systemic roots of male anger and low self-esteem, which men act out as violence against women and children and each other, and as violence between nations that are led by these same men.

"Low self-esteem, depression, and anger are not things that men are taught to handle. Kids learn that the best way to express anger is through being tough or violent, to abuse other people so you don't abuse yourself. I try to describe the cycle of how these young men were abused by their fathers, and they acted out against this other guy. So the attacker goes to jail and gets raped by men who probably came from a similar situation, and chances are when he gets out he'll be a perpetrator of more of the same kind of violence.

"People have asked me if the song is a reaction to

homophobia in rap music. While I condemn the blatantly homophobic lyrics in some rap music, 'Language of Violence' is a reaction to all of what's happening in our society—the whole attitude that it's acceptable to make fun of other people's sexuality."

From the outset, it was clear that Disposable Heroes of Hiphoprisy were different. First there was the matter of their name, which in a single breath addressed the transience of pop culture, the emptiness of hero worship, and the hypocrisy of hip-hop. Then there was the subject matter: in addition to gay-bashing, Franti took on OPEC, the excesses of the right-to-life movement, COINTELPRO, and the media's one-sided coverage of the U.S. invasion of Iraq. Where were the bitches and the hos, the hand grabbing the nuts, the bravado, and the violence? Is this the same rap that C. Delores Tucker and William Bennett were so upset about? (Perhaps they would have been even more unsettled if they'd listened to Franti's strong, thoughtful politics.)

As leader of the Disposable Heroes of Hiphoprisy, Franti helped usher a new phrase into the musical/political lexicon: artists of conscience. By the time the group released their album *Hypocrisy Is the Greatest Luxury*, it was high time that rap's compelling but often indiscriminate rage had a wider, more universal view. Especially because by the late 1980s, rappers (like rock stars before them) were being taken seriously as philosopher kings. Among their core base of fans, they were accorded the kind of respect once reserved for statesmen. Unfortunately, a lot of these emcees wielded influence way out of proportion to any political or social insight they might impart to their listeners. Ice Cube, for example, spent the early nineties telling audiences to read a spurious, anti-Semitic screed called *The Secret Relationship Between Blacks And Jews, Vol. 1*.

Less hateful but equally silly, KRS-One collected speaker's fees from Yale and Princeton to hold forth on the differences between technology and civilization.

As Franti points out, the fact that so many rappers were taken seriously as educators and leaders, both within and outside the black community, was at least partially because of the vacuum created by the assassination and imprisonment of the previous generation of black leaders. "There's a reason why rappers have been placed in the position of leadership for young black people in this country. In the sixties and seventies there was an effort by the CIA and the FBI to execute or incarcerate or force into exile all of the black leadership. That made it very easy for the Reagan-Bush administration to cut forty billion dollars in social spending, mostly from the black community, without any black leadership to cry out. So in the late eighties, you see a lot of young people using rap to attack government policies. The problem has been that many of these rappers aren't informed, so they're attacking symbols of authority rather than direct authority. On one hand, it's good that rap music has given young people a voice to express things politically, but on the other, some of the people who have been elevated to a leadership status don't understand what's going on in the world, and that's where you get this hypocrisy."

"It's important to realize that everybody's at a different level in their evolution and that we need to encourage everybody to keep going with it rather than to shut the door, 'cause there's validity in everybody's feelings. Sometimes we mask our feelings with our anger or by pointing the finger at other people, but the root is what our feelings are. Bob Marley said, 'Everybody thinks his burden is the heaviest. But who feels it knows it.' Unless we can really put ourselves in other people's places, we can't really understand what they're going through and feeling, why they're saying the things they say, and how they're reacting to the stimulus in their life."

Franti, who was adopted, didn't meet his birth parents until he was twenty-three years old. Born in Oakland and raised near Sacramento, he says he has felt like an outsider all his life. His adoptive parents were white but had adopted a mix of white and black children. They were also strict churchgoers. "I always felt like I marched to a different drummer than the people I was being raised by and with. As a kid I was always very rebellious. A lot of it came from the fact that I didn't get along well in my family. They were Lutheran and we went to church every Sunday, we prayed at every meal. They tried to keep me on a pretty tight leash and my whole life was a string of rebellions against that. Because I always felt like an outsider, I chose the side of the underdog in every situation."

Although the household was strict, music was not only allowed but encouraged. Ironically, Franti was the only member of the family who did not display an interest in music from an early age. "I had a brother who played trumpet, piano, guitar, harmonica, just about every instrument, and another brother who was a sax player. Both my sisters played violin and viola. My mom played organ in the church. We had a piano at home that was always being played by everybody. And I was . . . the ball player."

At six and a half feet tall, Franti was a gifted basketball player who attended the University of San Francisco on a basketball scholarship, and it was through his spoken word performances on the campus that his career as a musician began. His first group, the Beatnigs, grew out of an informal arrangement whereby some friends provided percussion accompaniment to his poems. "I just started playing with these two drummers, shouting my poetry on top of it. There was one guy who had a drum set, one who had congas, and another who did African percussion. We didn't have a place to rehearse, so we took the drums out to the shipyards; it would be real noisy out there so you could just play the drums and nobody gave a fuck. Gradually we started picking up things from the shipyards, scrap metal, old gas tanks, and barrel drums, and we started playing on them."

The Beatnigs were signed to Jello Biafra's Alternative Tentacles label and released an abrasive album of industrial noise in 1987. Early on, their music caught the attention of Billy Bragg, with whom they toured. Their shows included flying sparks triggered by an electric grinder brazing tire rims, and other homemade percussion sculptures made by Franti's partner, Rono Tse, whom he had met in San Francisco clubs. During performances with Disposable Heroes, Franti often lashed a microphoned piece of sheet metal with a thick length of chain while Tse scaled walls of speakers and brandished power tools.

Founded from the remnants of the Beatnigs, Disposable Heroes was a duo composed of Franti and Tse. "I found with the Beatnigs that the politics of the group frequently did not match up with how the band members conducted themselves in their personal lives—with their family, with their loved ones, with the people at the gigs," says Franti. "I saw that it's easy to say something in a song, and it's another thing to be responsible and put into action what you say. Disposable Heroes of Hiphoprisy was an effort, first, to recognize my own hypocrisy, as an artist of conscience in an industry that has no conscience, and second, to examine hypocrisy on a societal and world level. It's like Malcolm X—the thing that I gained from him is not his militancy but his ability to think critically and examine his life. That's where I feel we gain strength, through constantly conquering our own shortcomings and questioning our own beliefs."

Disposable Heroes of Hiphoprisy, however, did not survive. Franti and his longtime musical collaborator Rono Tse had increasingly divergent views on which way the music should go. Tse was more devoted to the group's industrial/punk past, while perhaps Franti was beginning to pay attention to reviewers who were more appreciative of his rapping than of the music, which at worst was perfunctory and at best still never set any dance floors on fire.

For Franti's next venture, an album called *Home* released under the name Spearhead, he enlisted the services of a producer with street credibility to spare—Joe "The Butcher" Nicolo, who had recently produced hit records for Cypress Hill. Nicolo's major innovation was in coaxing Franti, who has a deep, compelling voice but wobbly rap skills, to try his hand at singing. The album spawned two hits, "Hole in the Bucket" and "People in the Middle." Franti continued to tackle issues that most pop music steers clear of: "Positive," for example, addressed the fear of getting tested for AIDS. While his subject matter remained consistent, there was a difference between Franti's work with Disposable Heroes and Spearhead. It lay in his increasingly overt efforts to create beats that lived up to his lyrics: live music, played with a real band, that could move crowds instinctively as well as intellectually.

Chocolate Supa Highway, Franti's second effort with Spearhead, continued his search for music that people could bob their heads to. While this second album was far more listenable from a musical point of view than any of Disposable Heroes' work, it was also less distinctive; the weaker tracks verge on second-rate imitations of last year's R&B flavor of the month. In his attempt to deliver credible

and current beats, Franti ended up sounding slightly derivative, but the power of his lyrics remained undimin-
ished.

Every so often, the frustrations of the business side
of his career have made Franti think about throwing in
the towel. But several pivotal experiences have served to
remind him why he devoted his life to music and why his
music will always be about politics. "There have been times
when I wondered—and I still do regularly—what the fuck
am I doing in this business? When things get real crass
with the business side of it or when you see the sort of
glad-handing and back stabbing that goes on, you wonder,
could my energy be put to better use somewhere else? But
there have been some things that have helped me rededi-
cate myself to the type of work I do."

Franti recalls the day he was invited to speak at the
opening of a museum devoted to the history of slavery in
the city of Nantes, in France: "They had a model of what
it would be like to be in the bottom of a slave ship. I went
in there and lay down, and they put shackles on me and it
was dark and it was creaking and rocking; they had repro-
duced everything except the smell. I thought, what got
people through this journey? First of all, you had to have
faith in God. You had to have faith that there was a higher
power that was gonna guide and protect you. And second,
you had to have some sort of creative outlet so that you
wouldn't go crazy, and the only thing you could do on a
slave ship would be to sing songs. It dawned on me that
that was what has got us through as a people, our faith in
God and our creative expression, which has usually been
through music. That was one of the specific points in my
life where I rededicated myself to doing the type of music
that I do. I never sit down and go, I'm just gonna do a cool
hook and a fun song. I always sit down and ask, What am

I gonna try and say this time? What am I gonna do to tell a story and push the limits of where this music can go? That comes from a lot of soul-searching."

Toward the end of a 1992 tour in which Disposable Heroes opened for U2, Franti had an encounter with Bono that taught him another lesson about the role a songwriter can play in society, on the most practical level. "Bono told me he had gone to Africa to dig ditches and help the poverty-stricken Africans. His wife was with him and they were, like, the only two white people in this village. After the first day of digging ditches, his hands were all tired and sore, and he went back to his little hut, feeling really good, like he just did something good and real. And the villagers came up to him and they said, 'Mr. Bono, respectfully, we appreciate the hard work you did today, but you pretty much set us back a few days in our efforts to make this well, and you suck at being a ditchdigger.' They said, 'Don't think that we're ignorant out here and don't know that you're from this group U2 and that you're a songwriter. We really respect songwriters in our village and we could use some songs.' So—the village was having a problem with the water, so they wrote a song called 'You Boil Water before You Drink It' and another one called, 'Don't Put Cow Dung On a Baby's Umbilical Cord,' which referred to the use of dung as an antiseptic, which was no longer effective because of the tainted water. Bono's wife made up little hand signals for the songs and taught them to the kids, and they became part of the village's oral history.

"It suddenly dawned on me, through that story, that when you have the gift of storytelling and songwriting, there is a responsibility that goes along with it, even when you're working in the pop world. Sometimes you think it's silly and meaningless, but at the end of the day, if you put your heart into your songs, people feel it. For ten years I've made records that a relatively small number of people have heard, but they e-mail me and write me letters and come up to me after shows and talk to me for hours. I feel like I'm doin' something that has meaning for other people, something that's important and comes through a creative spirit that I'm not always in control of.

"I was always taught the golden rule at home and in the classroom, but I never truly grasped the concept until I met my grandma for the first time, when I was twenty-three years old. My grandma said, 'Be nice to who be's nice to you.' The first time we met she said that to me, and she said it again and again till she died last Christmas. The way she said it, just, 'Be nice to who be's nice to you,' made it so much simpler and clearer to me. She had been raised by her own grandmother, who had been a slave until she was twelve, and she worked as a domestic her whole life. She wiped people's asses, she took care of sick people, she mopped floors, she did everything. For her to have lived through all those things and still say, 'Be nice to who be's nice to you,' it moved me. It was a very powerful thing."

Fanti's songs are rarely explicit in their treatment of spiritual themes, but in his personal life, the search for a transcendent meaning has never subsided. Although he long ago lost touch with the Lutheran Church of his childhood, he has continued to make prayer a part of his daily life. "I always had my own connection with God and I prayed every night as long as I can remember. I still do to this day. When I was little I would pray a lot to find my parents. Usually what I pray for now—a practice that I started at around eighteen or nineteen—is just for guidance and protection. It is kind of my own personal thing, but it has always been the foundation of my music, too."

Franti's love affair with socially conscious music dates back to his encounter with the Jamaican poet Linton Kwesi Johnson in 1981. "I went to see Linton Kwesi Johnson, I was about fourteen, and this little dude walks onto the stage with glasses and a little suit on and a hat, and he just read this song called 'Sonny's Lettah.' He did it a cappella, and five hundred people just stood there, totally captivated. I said, That's what I want to do. The poem was about a young man writing to his mom from jail, about how he had killed a cop who had started to dump on his little brother because they were in a neighborhood where there weren't a lot of black people. This was in England. From that point on I wanted to write songs that make people feel emotions but are about larger social issues. That's what I set out to do.

"Questions of race and identity have always been at the forefront of my consciousness. That's one of the reasons I was attracted to reggae music, because it put blackness in the front. Through Rasta, black pride was being expressed in the music, and the connection to God and faith. Even though there's a belief in God, Rastas will tell you it's not a religion, it's just a way of life."

Although Franti often makes reference to Rastafarianism ("guidance and protection" is a common Rasta phrase), it was his 1992 encounter with the Maoris, the indigenous people of New Zealand, that had the greatest impact on his spiritual development. "I went down to New Zealand to perform, and I met somebody walking down the street who didn't look white. I said to him, 'I wanna find out what's goin' on with the indigenous people here,' and he said, 'Cool, I'll hook you up with some people.' He introduced me to a traditional carver named George Nuku, who explained to me how carving was the way the Maori documented their history and that the carver in their tribe is the storyteller. He taught me a lot about Maori spirituality."

In the Maori language there is a concept called *kulpepa*, which is something like the idea of the Tao, meaning one's natural path in life. "It's like each person has two sets of footsteps: you have your spiritual footsteps and you have your functional footsteps. The functional footsteps are how we live in Babylon, the things we have to do for money, like get jobs, go to work. The key is to try to match the imprints of your functional footsteps with your spiritual footsteps. And so I have a *kulpepa*, I have a way of life, a destination. I have a guiding light that compels me and I have protection that propels me along the way. I don't really identify with one religious order, but I do believe in God and I do have a path that I follow."

Franti returned to New Zealand the following year to perform a benefit to raise money for *wakas*, the Maoris' traditional canoes. "They get the different gangs in the community to build canoes and then race them. We went to raise money for them, and when we got there they gave us a traditional Maori greeting, which is called a *haka*. It's a very heavy, intense greeting. The women come out and sing these very beautiful songs and the men come out and blow conch shells. They invite you into their space, they welcome you to their land. The men do this ferocious dance and chant these superloud chants. They do a set regimen of warrior movements. And then they shout all these things and make crazy faces with their tongues out, and what they're saying could be literally translated as, 'I could cut your head off, crack your skull, and suck your brains out. I could fuck you up and do all this shit to you,' but then they say, 'But we're not gonna do it to you.' They practice it as a combat thing, but it's theatrical and representational, and what would happen traditionally is that one tribe would meet up with another tribe, and they would shout at each other, they would curse the other tribe out. It's like puffing your chest to say, 'We could fuck you up but we're not going to, and you're welcome to come in, but just know that we could have done this to you.' "

The Maoris' welcome of Franti is interesting in its similarity to the tradition of braggadocio in hip-hop, but if they were looking for a rapper who would respond by puffing up his own chest, Franti was not the one. Instead he responded with a song, sung a cappella, about the emptiness of fame and wealth. "It was my obligation to respond to them, but since they did that whole thing in Maori, I didn't know what to say, so I just did one of my songs. It was 'Famous and Dandy like Amos and Andy.' I later wrote a song called 'Of Course You Can,' which was inspired by being there.

"One thing I've found as I've gone around the world is that there are black people in every culture. Even aboriginal people like the Maori identify themselves as black. Everywhere you go in the colonized world there's this whole network of people who have a connection to God and to the soil, and I guess I identify with that spirit. That's what I called Spearhead's second album, *Chocolate Supa Highway*.

"Wherever you go, there's gonna be people who have been stepped down on, and there's some people who are still fighting for their liberation today. The bottom line is, there's justice and injustice. The development of love, balance, harmony, and understanding are issues we have to deal with each day. But we also have to make a distinction between power and authority. Who has power and who has authority? All of us hold the power. We're the people who work, who have the creative energy, the juice, the love, and I don't just mean black people, I mean all people who go about their lives every day. Each of us has power, yet there have been a few people who have been able to convince us that they have authority. They erect monuments to it and they create governments for it and legal systems that are totally unjust. They've created money and all these other things that feed the illusion that they have authority over us.

"One of the things that God and spirituality bring to us is the ability to get in touch with where the real power is, which is in the hearts of each of us and in our ability to go about daily life. Everybody suffers some form of injustice, some problem, gets hurt, gets old and dies. We should have compassion for everybody in the world and we should fight for justice for everybody in the world. What I try to do through my music is to get people back in touch with their power, and in turn to show up authority for the wizard behind the curtain that it really is."

NUSRAT FATEH ALI KHAN

A Tradition of Ecstasy

Nusrat Fateh Ali Khan is a soft-spoken man. Despite his ability to sing in a voice of wrenching power, in person his words tumble out in whispers, disappearing into his ample chest. The Pakistani-born singer is South Asia's most popular musician, with a voice that coils upward like a snake being charmed out of a basket, raising listeners to a kind of spiritual ecstasy. He is perhaps the world's greatest master of qawwali, a mystical Sufi music, which literally means utterance, or saying. Qawwali is among the forms of music in which religion and sex seem most closely intertwined, and the Sufis have traditionally expressed their devotion to Allah using sex and drunkenness as key metaphors. When Nusrat Fateh Ali Khan sings qawwali, his voice, accompanied by a party of tabla drummers and harmonium players, has a quavering orgasmic quality that drives listeners wild, causing them to shower him with money and dance in a manner most unacceptable to the ayatollahs of this world.

Although Khan is not a particularly tall man, he weighs several hundred pounds and has a protuberant midsection that's difficult not to notice. But his delicate hands, ending in wispy fingertips, look like they belong on a little girl. One finger is adorned by a jade ring the size of a grape. His watch, a sleek black-and-gold number by Cartier, would be at home on the wrist of an oil-producing sheikh. His eyebrows are barely existent, and he has a giant, smooth forehead with fiery eyes weirdly planted a bit higher in the skull than normal.

Although Khan has recorded more than a hundred albums and enjoyed widespread popularity in Pakistani communities around the world for many years, Western audiences only discovered his work after Peter Gabriel performed live with Khan and helped distribute his albums in the West. More recently, Eddie Vedder of Pearl Jam sought Khan out for a collaboration that appeared on the sound track to *Dead Man Walking*.

A few days after attending the 1996 MTV Video Music Awards with Peter Gabriel, Khan sat down with me in a dimly lit lounge of a hotel in midtown Manhattan, attended by an interpreter and his manager. As his vast corpulence settled into the couch, his beige gown draping the floor, he seemed at once kingly, unearthly, and decidedly out of place in the middle of New York. There in the shadows, rocking his girth from side to side, Khan spoke softly and without any hint of his awesome lung power, his presence largely unnoticed by passersby unaware of the qawwali master in their midst.

Although Khan's music is based entirely on the Sufi tradition, an offshoot of Islam that emphasizes mystical and often poetic expression of the divine, he is circumspect about his personal religious affiliation. "I am not Sufi," Khan says, "but I spent a lot of time from my childhood up until now with the Sufis and I deeply studied them. Sufi music is a kind of prayer, and if you sing in this manner, you will become closer to God, very close. That's basically what I do. Every religion has its own way of describing God. Buddhism, Hinduism, Christianity, Sikhism—they all have their own way of following God. Sufism describes

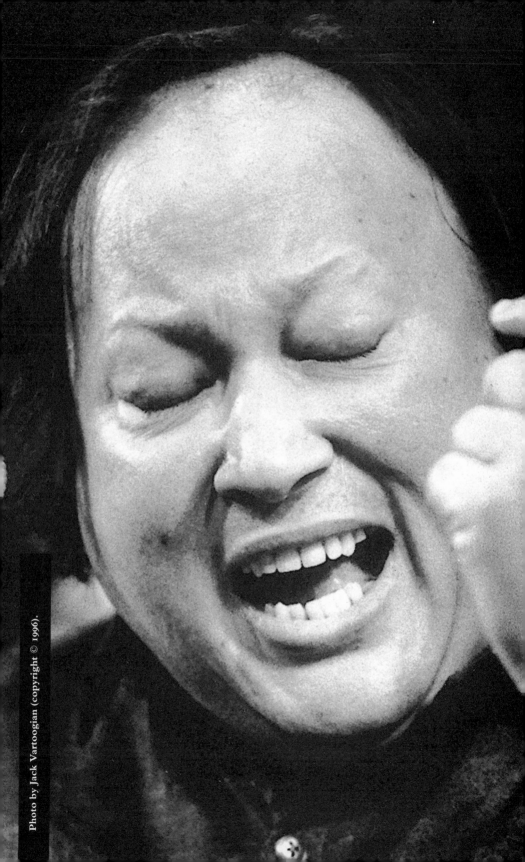

God and teaches how to come closer to God. So basically, I follow the Islamic form of Sufism to find my way to God."

According to Sufism, the voice is indicative not only of a man's character but also of his spirit, the degree of his spiritual evolution. Sufis believe that no word uttered is ever lost, that the sound reverberates into the cosmos infinitely, according to the spirit put into it. In the Sufi view, music and spirit are inextricably intertwined, as the great Sufi teacher Inayat Khan wrote in his book *Music*:

> Music is a miniature of the harmony of the whole universe, for the harmony of the universe is life itself, and man, being a miniature of the universe, shows harmonious or inharmonious chords in his pulsation, in the beat of his heart, in his vibration, rhythm and tone. His health or illness, his joy or discomfort, all show the music or lack of music in his life.
>
> Where does music come from? Where does the dance come from? It all comes from that natural and spiritual life which is within. When that spiritual life springs forth, it lightens all the burdens that man has. It makes his life smooth, as though floating on the ocean of life.

When Nusrat Fateh Ali Khan performs, his hands seem to float on the surface of unseen waves. His wrists move in a dancerly fashion, describing small arcs and pirouettes, his fingers extended in a manner reminiscent of classical Indian dance. His face reflects an absorption that cannot be faked, as he reflects on the personalities of Allah, Muhammad, and the Sufi saints. Khan's performances are like public prayer sessions, during which he calls to mind through qawwali singing the nature of the sacred Muslim figures.

"When I sing traditional spiritual songs, I always

concentrate on who it is that I'm singing about. For instance, if I am inspired by the Holy Prophet, I concentrate on the Prophet. When I sing, I sing for God and for holy prophets, and their personalities are in my mind. Accordingly, whenever I sing about God, or the prophet Muhammad, I feel like I am in front of him. I feel their personalities, and I pray.

"I feel like I am in another world when I sing, the spiritual world. I am not in the material world while I am singing these traditional holy messages. I'm totally in another world. I am withdrawn from my materialistic senses, I am totally in my spiritual senses, and I am intoxicated by the Holy Prophet, God, and other Sufi saints.

"When I sing for God, I feel myself in accord with God. The house of God, Mecca, is right in front of me, and I worship. When I sing for Muhammad, peace be upon him, our prophet, I feel like I am sitting right next to his tomb, Medina, and paying him respect and admitting to myself that I accept his message. When I sing about the Sufi saints, I feel like the saints are in front of me, and as a student, I am accepting their teachings. I repeat again and again that I accept their teachings, that I am really their follower."

Sufism, a Muslim philosophical and literary movement dating back to the tenth century, requires that adherents make a direct connection with the divine, often through poetry or, in the case of qawwali, through music. Qawwali is traditionally passed on from father to son (and in very rare cases to daughters). In Khan's case, his father, Ustad Fateh Ali Khan, a great qawwali singer, died before initiating his son into the tradition, but shortly after his father's death, in 1964, Khan had a visionary dream. In the dream, Khan's father came to him and told him that he had been given his musical gift and should devote his life to qawwali. He touched his son's throat, and Khan started to sing. He woke up singing, and at his father's funeral ceremony on the fortieth day after his death, he performed for the first time.

Since that time, Khan has grown not only as a singer but in his understanding of the deep message that his songs express. "Since the age of sixteen, when I started singing, I have had the same message to deliver to people about Sufism, as my experiences grew. Of course you go to greater depths as time passes, and you grow and grow with the songs. My message is the message of humanity: love and peace. The goal is to bring people toward brotherhood, to bring them closer to each other, without hatred, without any concern for race, religion, or color. I try to bring people, through spirituality, to a position in which they'll be more honest with each other, and live a truer life, less concerned with the materialistic world where they cannot find themselves. I try to bring them to a place where they can at least recognize themselves."

In addition to his musical practice, which has a very powerful spiritual dimension, Khan also has a formal religious practice. "I pray five times a day. I pray before I eat, giving thanks to my God for the opportunity to eat this food; and after eating, I pray and give thanks again. After all of my practices of my music, I always pray and give thanks to my God and say, God, I am your slave, and thanks to you I have this opportunity to give my message to the world.

"During the time I am singing traditional qawwali songs, I feel that I am in a prayer position in front of God. When I finish my prayers, whether is it my singing or the formal prayers I do five times a day, I feel deeply peaceful. I feel that I have had some success in accomplishing the mission that God has given me. I have no difficulty making a transition from that frame of mind, when I am singing, to my normal daily activities, because prayer is a routine part of my life and I do it all the time. Because of this music and this message that we have in our hearts and our minds all the time, it is extremely rare to feel anger toward anybody. This is the basic medication that controls us, preventing us from getting angry, and keeps us happy."

Much of the singer's lifestyle is based on tradition, passed down from his ancestors to his great-grandparents, and from his parents directly to him. "From my parents I learned my religion, how to live, how to follow Islamic rules. When I was young I went to the mosque and read the Koran and learned all the Islamic rules. From my teachers I got an education in science, mathematics, geography, English, Urdu, all the common subjects. And from Sufis, I learned about Sufism. I try to integrate the teachings from these three sources, from the saints, from school, and from my father. Of course, when I was a child, before I turned sixteen, I was just a regular young person. I got angry, I argued, I lived like a boy. But since I saw the dream and became a follower of Sufism, and began singing the traditional qawwali, it really gave me peace in my heart. Since then my life has been totally changed, and I control everything that comes to my brain and to my heart."

While the spiritual elements in Khan's music are paramount, that has not prevented him from being rather successful on the material plane. He has sold more than a million albums worldwide, and his music has been included on sound tracks for movies such as *Last Temptation of Christ*, *Dead Man Walking*, and *Natural Born Killers*. The sudden influx of money associated with such popularity can complicate any musician's life, but although he lives today in an expensive suburb of Lahore, Khan says that his concern with material success has steadily waned over the years. "When I started singing, of course I had in my mind the desire for success. I was always thinking that the people should listen to me, that the crowd should pay me respect as the artist. I wanted applause and felt that the singer should get some reward in the shape of appreciation from the public. But as time went by, I found myself in a situation where all I wanted is to give a lesson, the purpose of which is to give more happiness to people. My sleeping, my waking, my talking, my eating—throughout my life, the music is always with me in my mind."

Author's Note: On August 16, 1997, just a few weeks before this book was printed, Nusrat Fateh Ali Khan died of a heart attack at Cromwell hospital in London. He was 49 years old.

ALLEN GINSBERG
That Which Is Vivid

ALLEN GINSBER

"I began in the shower, as a kid," Allen Ginsberg said, but America's most celebrated modern poet wasn't talking about writing poems. We spoke a few months before he died, at the age of seventy, in the spring of 1997, and he was talking about his *other* career, one less well known, which spanned several decades and included a prodigious output in collaboration with Bob Dylan, Philip Glass, the Clash, Paul McCartney, and other eminent musicians. "Like everybody else, I started by singing in the shower. I had some favorite singers, like Leadbelly. I loved him singing 'Black Girl, Black Girl,' that song Kurt Cobain covered later in the MTV *Unplugged* series. I used to sing that when I was in grammar school and high school because Leadbelly had a half-hour radio program on WNYC once a week.

"So I grew up on Leadbelly, and I lived in a slum area of Paterson, New Jersey, near the river where there were a lot of black spiritual churches. As a little kid, five or six years old, I used to wander into them. They were kind and welcoming, and sat me down in the pew, and I'd listen to all this gorgeous call-and-response music. So I had a lot of music in my childhood. My mother played mandolin and I took some violin and piano lessons, but I never learned anything."

In 1944, long before his interest in music approached anything resembling a profession, Ginsberg met Jack Kerouac and William Burroughs in New York, forming a literary and philosophical triumvirate that would give rise to the Beat movement.

The birth of the Beats was coemergent with the golden age of bebop, and Ginsberg spent a lot of time connecting the two worlds. "With Kerouac, in the forties, I used to go around to clubs and listen to Charlie Parker and Thelonious Monk and Lester Young. I spent a lot of time at the Five Spot, listening to them."

Another person Ginsberg spent a lot of time with during this period was Harry Smith, an ethnomusicologist and producer who assembled an influential three-volume, six-record anthology of American folk music, which he released on Folkways Records in 1952. "That album set the stage for and inspired the folk revival of the fifties," Ginsberg said. "A lot of the songs on Dylan's first record were collected by Harry, and Jerry Garcia also learned a lot about blues from Harry's anthology.

"Harry recorded an album of my first blues on an old Wollensak in the Chelsea Hotel in 1971 that was edited by Sam Charters, a blues scholar who ran Portense Records. So I've had a lot of connection to the blues through Sam and Harry, who was indigent and alcoholic for some time, so he stayed with me. I brought Harry out to Naropa Institute, where he became a favorite philosopher in residence. People would go and smoke pot and consult him about American Indian anthropological matters or ethnomusicological matters, or hermetics, the tarot, that sort of thing."

As the 1950s drew to a close, Ginsberg began to move into the realm of sacred music, reflecting both a newly emergent Eastern influence and his enduring obsession with the poet William Blake. "Beginning with my time

in India in 1963, I began doing a lot of mantra chanting, and for many years I prefaced my poetry readings with either Buddhist or Hindu chants. I used to travel around with Ram Dass and read poetry and do some chanting with him, and I developed a voice that way, through sacred music.

"In the late sixties, I began setting William Blake's *Songs of Innocence and of Experience* to music, accompanying them on a harmonium. The harmonium was similar to the instruments that he played in his day, which were a parlor organ or a harmonium; the reason they're called songs, according to his biographers, is that Blake sang them. I had a little miniature Indian harmonium that I used, which could give you three or four chords and two and a half octaves. In 1969, I made recordings of twenty-two of Blake's songs. I didn't know much music, I just knew one chord. But when I came back from the Chicago '68 convention, I was in a kind of state of shock and Blake was the only one who made sense."

When the time came for Ginsberg to enter the recording studio, he took advantage of his connection to the jazz greats he had met years earlier at the Five Spot; Charles Mingus, in particular, helped Ginsberg assemble the cast of bebop luminaries who would form his band for the Blake recordings.

"I had known Mingus for years, and had in fact sung at his wedding, because I was into Indian music and chanting at the time. Indian music is modal, and many of the jazz geniuses like Mingus and John Coltrane were interested in that modal style. So I consulted Charlie Mingus, who was a neighbor, and he suggested musicians, and I made a recording with Don Cherry, Elvin Jones, and a few other musicians that Mingus had suggested.

"We sold it to MGM, but in 1970 some Las Vegas

billionaire gangster bought the company and did some sort of hypocritical thing, saying that they would not work with anyone who took drugs, so my album was sort of buried."

In the late sixties, Ginsberg's music shifted slightly in a more popular direction. In Bob Dylan he found a musical mentor who helped him focus on the rudiments of pop song craft. "I began transferring my affections to folk music, and Dylan showed me the three-chord blues pattern for ballads. I went out with Dylan on the Rolling Thunder tour; I was sort of like the house philosopher and poet, and I also played in the percussion section occasionally with finger cymbals and once in a while read poetry in the intermissions.

"When I got back, I did a lot of recording of my own songs, inspired by Happy Traum and Dylan and Harry Smith's compilations. I also put out a book called *First Blues*. John Hammond Sr. recorded some of that material for Columbia, but they wouldn't have it because some of those words were too dirty. Like I had an anti-smoking song that said: 'Don't smoke / don't smoke / it's a nine billion dollar capitalist / communist joke / suck tit, suck cock, suck clit, but don't smoke shit / nope, nope, nope, it's too obscene that nicotine.' Hammond thought it was great, but Columbia was scared to put it out. Hammond got his own label in 1984 and he put out a double album called *First Blues* with a cover photo by Robert Frank, including songs I did with Dylan, the original 1975 Hammond tapes, and the stuff I did in '81."

In the late eighties, Ginsberg began working with Hal Wilner, the musical director at *Saturday Night Live*, who assembled a band of superb musicians for Ginsberg, including Marc Ribot, Bill Frisell, Steve Swallow, and Lenny Pickett, and produced *The Lion for Real* (Island Records).

"That was the first time I didn't produce my own recording and it was the first time I did spoken poetry with jazz. Each musician chose a text out of my collected works and figured out their treatment and then they came in and we recorded it together."

Ginsberg's next major musical project was the *Hydrogen Jukebox* opera created in collaboration with Philip Glass (Nonesuch/Elektra). He was increasingly doing projects far removed from his folksy bardic beginnings. As testimony to the breadth of musical territory his work had encompassed, Rhino Records released a four-CD retrospective in 1994, including both music and poems, called *Holy Soul Jelly Roll, Poems and Songs 1949–1993*. The set features the earliest song Ginsberg recorded, taped on a home machine with Kerouac in New York in 1949.

As Stephen Prothero noted in his introduction to *Big Sky Mind*, from the outset the Beats were united by a distinctly spiritual quest for a new consciousness, rather than by any shared political views or literary style. Prothero wrote, "When Allen Ginsberg was asked, 'Were the Beats first and foremost artists or first and foremost spiritual seekers?' he saw the trap and refused to enter. The two, he answered, are inseparable, and he cited the example of the Milarepa school of Tibetan Buddhism, where in order to become a lama one must reportedly also be an archer, a calligrapher, or a poet. 'The life of poetry,' he added, is 'a sacramental life on earth.' "

While Ginsberg has described himself as a Buddhist Jew, and Judaism has remained an essential part of his identity as an artist (one of his most famous poems, *Kaddish*, takes its name from the Jewish mourning prayer), in the 1970s he developed a formal commitment to Buddhism, followed by years of serious study and practice. During a 1993 Jewel Heart retreat, in Ann Arbor, Ginsberg gave a lecture outlining the major points in his spiritual evolution. "In 1948 I had some kind of break in the normal modality of my consciousness. While alone living a relatively solitary vegetarian contemplative life, I had an extraordinary break in the normal nature of my thought, when something opened up.

"I had finished masturbating, actually, on the sixth floor of a Harlem tenement on 121st Street looking out at the roofs while reading Blake, and suddenly had a kind of auditory hallucination, hearing Blake—what I thought was his voice, very deep, earthen tone, not very far from my own mature tone of voice, so perhaps a projection of my own latent physiology—reciting a poem called 'The Sunflower,' which I thought expressed some kind of universal longing for union with some infinite nature. The poem goes, 'Ah, Sunflower / Weary of time / Who counteth the steps of the sun / Seeking after that sweet golden clime where the traveler's journey is done / Where the youth pined away with desire / And the pale virgin shrouded with snow / Arise from their graves and aspire where my sunflower wishes to go.'

"I can't interpret it exactly now, but the impression I had at the time was of some infinite yearning for the infinite, finally realized, and I looked out the window and began to notice the extraordinary detail of intelligent labor that had gone into the making of the rooftop cornices of the Harlem buildings. And I suddenly realized that the world was, in a sense, not dead matter but an increment or deposit of living intelligence and action and activity that finally took form.

"And as I looked at the sky, I wondered what kind of intelligence had made that vastness, or what was the nature of the intelligence that I was glimpsing, and felt a sense of vastness and of coming home to a space I hadn't realized was there before but which seemed old and infinite, like the Ancient of Days, so to speak.

"But I had no training in anything but Western notions and didn't know how to find a vocabulary for the experience, so I thought I had seen 'God' or 'Light' or some Western notion of a theistic center, or that was the impression at the time.

"That got me into lots of trouble because I tried to explain it to people and nobody could figure out what I was saying; they thought I was nuts, and in a way, I was. Having no background and no preparation, I didn't know how to ground the experience in any way that could either prolong it or put it in its place, and I certainly didn't know any teachers whom I could have consulted at Columbia at the time, although D. T. Suzuki was there.

"By 1950 or 1951, because of those experiences, I was curious about the Tibetan *thangkas*, which depicted wrathful deities, but I had no idea what their functions were. I also began experimenting more with peyote and other psychedelics—mescaline and later LSD—to see if I could approximate the natural experience I'd had. My experience with them was very similar, although the natural experience was much more ample and left a deeper imprint on my nature, and it certainly turned me around at the age of twenty-two."

"By 1950 Kerouac had begun reading Buddhist texts, in reaction to our friend Neal Cassady, who was involved with Edgar Cayce, a sort of channeling specialist somewhat famous in those years. Kerouac thought this was a crude, provincial American 'Billy Sunday in a suit,' so maybe he should go back to the original text relating to metempsychosis and reincarnation. So Kerouac began reading Dwight Goddard's *Buddhist Bible*, which had samples of Hinayana and Mahayana texts, including the *Dia-*

mond Sutra, and some Vajrayana texts, at least relating to Milarepa and others. And he laid that trip on me.

"Now as an ex-Communist Jewish intellectual, I thought his pronouncement of the first noble truth, that existence was suffering, was some sort of insult to my left-wing background, since I was a progressive looking forward to the universal improvement of matters, if only through spiritual advancement. Kerouac's insistence was that existence contained suffering. I thought he was just trying to insult me, for some reason or other. It took me about two years to get it through my head that he was just telling me a very simple fact."

Ginsberg's first instruction in Buddhist teaching came from Kerouac, who tried to explain the Buddhist concept of emptiness to him. "The first time I heard the refuge vows was from Kerouac also, crooned like Frank Sinatra in a very beautiful way. So that imprinted itself on me, and I began going to the New York Public Library and looking at Chinese paintings of the Sung dynasty, interested in the vastness of the landscape scrolls, as correlating with the sense of vastness that I had already experienced."

In 1962, after a trip to Europe, Ginsberg went to India to look for a teacher. "By then I was quite well known as a poet, and I figured that the proper move, being now famous, would be to disappear into India for a couple of years and look for some wisdom, and also experience a different culture than the Western culture, which I thought from the viewpoint of Spengler, the *Decline of the West,* was perhaps exhausted of inspiration and it was time for a second religiousness, and so I went to look for a teacher. I went in company with Gary Snyder, who four years earlier had gone to Kyoto to study at the first Zen institute at Daitoku-ji monastery and had begun helping translate *Zen Dust,* a handbook of koans.

"We went on a Buddhist pilgrimage to Sarnath, Sanchi, Ajanta, Ellora. In a cave at Ellora, Gary sat himself down and chanted the *Prajnaparamita-sutra* in Sino-Japanese, with echoes of the cave around, and that blew my mind. That was such an extended, long, and obviously spiritual breath, vocalized, that I got really interested and began to ask him about what it meant and why he was doing it in Japanese, and what the history of it was.

"I went on to Kalimpong to visit Dudjom Rinpoche, the head of the Nyingma school, and I brought him my problems with LSD, because I had a lot of bum trips. Every time I took acid or psychedelics, I would come back to 'The Sick Rose,' like some kind of monster coming to eat me from an outside space. And he did give me a very good pith instruction, which I never forgot. It turned my mind around and made the world safe for my democratic thoughts: 'If you see something horrible, don't cling to it, and if you see something beautiful, don't cling to it.' That cut the Gordian knot that I'd inherited from too rash and untutored experiments with psychedelics.

"On my way home I went to Japan and visited Gary, and sat at Daitoku-ji Temple, and actually did a short *sesshin* but didn't learn anything because I didn't get any real instructions. The problem I had in India was that I didn't know what to ask for. I went there looking for a teacher and I saw many swamis, but I didn't know enough to ask them for a meditation practice. Which was the simplest way in? What kind of meditation do you do, and can you suggest a practice? I just was too dumb to know that. I remember asking Dudjom Rinpoche for initiations, *wang*, as if I were trained enough or prepared for it, but I didn't ask him what kind of meditation I should practice meanwhile."

It was his encounter with the controversial Tibetan

teacher Chögyam Trungpa Rinpoche, with whom Ginsberg took formal refuge in Buddhism in May 1972, that
would have the most impact on his work, changing his understanding of the creative process and inspiring many
songs and poems with specifically Buddhist themes. At
Trungpa's request, Ginsberg cofounded the Jack Kerouac
School of Disembodied Poetics at Trungpa's Buddhist university, the Naropa Institute, in Boulder, Colorado.

His first meeting with Trungpa was a chance encounter on the streets of Manhattan, when Ginsberg attempted to commandeer a taxi from the lama. Retelling
the tale, Ginsberg saw symbolic relevance in the fact that
the first words he spoke to his future teacher were: "May I
borrow your vehicle?" (In Buddhist terminology, the
teachings are often referred to as vehicles.)

"In 1970 Gary Snyder had a book party in New
York. My father had never met Gary and I figured this was
a good opportunity. After the party I was taking him to
Port Authority to get a bus to Paterson. We started walking,
but it was a very hot day and my father was in his seventies
at the time and beginning to fade a little. So, passing on
43rd street by Town Hall, I saw a taxi stop for an Oriental
guy and I stepped up and said, 'Excuse me, my father is
ill. May I steal your vehicle?' And the guy with him said,
'Oh, you're Allen Ginsberg.' And I said, 'Yeah.' And he
said, 'This is the Venerable Chögyam Trungpa Rinpoche.'
So I made a *namaste* and said '*Om ah hum vajra guru padma
siddhi hum*.' So he saw that my father was ill and said, 'Of
course.'

"About a month or two later, I got an invitation to
visit with Trungpa Rinpoche at a tiny apartment on the
Lower East Side. We sat down and Kunga Dawa, at Trungpa's side, offered me a joint of marijuana—skillful means,
I thought—and I was amazed that Trungpa was that much

of a bohemian, or that supple minded. So I smoked a little—he didn't but Kunga did—and then he gave me the 'Sadhana of Mahamudra,' a long, very beautiful devotional poem that he had written. He asked me to read it aloud. I think it was a way of sort of hooking me in. I was very moved by his manner, his intelligence, his humor in providing me with the joint and just his willingness to be open.

"And a while later, in 1971, we had a really interesting meeting in San Francisco. I had made a date to meet at his motel. When I got there, everybody was late, and then I heard a noise outside, and I saw him with two disciples, stumbling totally drunk up the stairs. He was so drunk that his pants got caught on a nail and ripped. He got into the room, and his wife was angry at him—she had a new little baby—and pissed off that he was drunk in the middle of the afternoon.

"I sat down with my harmonium. I saw his itinerary of talks and asked, 'Don't you get tired of that?' I was on the road, and I was getting a little bored, fatigued, traveling. He said, 'That's because you don't like your poetry.' I said, 'What do you know about poetry?' He said, 'Why don't you do like the great poets do, like Milarepa? You're bored with reading the same poems over and over. Why don't you make poems up on the stage? Why do you need a piece of paper? Don't you trust your own mind?'

"Actually, that was very good advice, the same advice given me by Kerouac many years before. It was right in the groove of everything I had been learning but coming from another direction entirely—the insight or mind consciousness of a well-trained meditator and specialist, a kind of genius meditator.

"Then I showed him mantras I had been chanting and playing and he put his paw, drunk, on the harmonium keys and said, 'Remember, the silence is just as important as the sound.'

"We went out to supper and got more drunk, and he said, 'Why are you hiding your face? I'd like to see your face. Why do you have that big beard?' I had a big sixties beard, hung over into the seventies, and I said, 'If you'll stop drinking, I'll shave my beard right this minute.' I went into the drugstore, bought a razor and shaved my beard. And I came back and said, 'Now you've got to stop drinking.' And he said, 'That's another matter. You didn't shave your beard completely.' Because it was still in rough tufts.

"We went off to his lecture and I remember he was sitting very sadly in a chair, talking to this group of San Francisco hippies, saying, 'No more trips, please, no more trips, no more trips.' Meaning whatever, acid, but also spiritual materialist trips, the accumulation of Blakian experiences for the purpose of impressing other people as credentials of one's own sanctity or accomplishment. It was probably the series of lectures called 'Buddhadharma without Credentials.'

"At this lecture I continued shaving, and I came back out again, and he asked me to improvise. 'This is Allen Ginsberg, the great poet. Now we are going to have him improvise.' I couldn't think of anything: 'Here we are in the middle of June / I just ate with you and I had a spoon / and we were talking about the moon.' Actually, walking on the way over he'd said, 'America is not ready for the full moon,' meaning full doctrine, I think, full dharma. And I said, 'That shouldn't dismay the moon.'

"So I tried improvising but I didn't do very well, and he said, 'You're too smart.' But the next day I had a regular poetry reading at the Berkeley Community Theater as a benefit for Tarthang Tulku. So I resolved that I would go onstage without any paper at all, but I did bring the harmonium and improvised something like:

" 'How sweet to be born in America where we have like a *deva-loka* where the god world is here and we have all the watermelons we want to eat and everybody else is starving around the world, but how sweet to be here in the heaven world which may last for a little bit of time but how sweet to be born.' It was a bittersweet song; it's still at the height of the war. So it's 'How sweet to be born in America, where we're dropping bombs on somebody else but not on ourselves.'

"I've forgotten because it was improvised, but it actually did me a lot of good, his prompting, because from then on I was never scared to get up onstage even if I'd left my poetry back on the train or something. It was always a workable situation from then on.

"Then when I went out to Colorado in 1972, he invited me to help him raise some money for Rocky Mountain Dharma Center, so I gave a reading with him, Gary Snyder, Robert Bly, and Nanao Sakaki, a Japanese poet I like, in a big hall at the University of Colorado. First Robert Bly read. Trungpa was drunk, as ever, but while Bly was reading, he did something very strange. He picked up the big gong and he put it over his head while Bly was reading. Bly couldn't see because we were all lined up parallel, so he didn't see what was going on there. The audience was tittering a little bit, and I leaned over and said to Trungpa, 'You shouldn't do that, they're making a benefit for you, they've come here to do you a favor, you shouldn't be carrying on like that.' And he said, 'If you think I'm doing this because I'm drunk, you're making a big mistake.'

"Then Gary Snyder read, and while he was reading Trungpa Rinpoche took the gong and put it on *my* head.

So I just sat there figuring, well, he must know what he's doing, or if he doesn't, I don't, so I'm not going to get in the way. I'm not the host, I don't have to worry about it, though Gary was a friend of mine. After it was over then I read, and he didn't do anything while I read. I asked later why not and he said, 'Because you don't know what you're doing.'

"A couple of weeks later I asked him why he did that, and he said, 'Well, Bly was presenting Robert Bly—a big ham, so to speak. Gary Snyder was presenting Gary Snyder as sort of the finished Zen product. You know, neat and perfect and proper shoes and all that.' He said that the people in the audience were his students and he didn't want them to get the wrong idea of what was the ideal version of a poet. Later he wrote a spontaneous poem saying Robert Bly presented Robert Bly, Gary Snyder presented Gary Snyder, Ginsberg was Ginsberg, but only Trungpa was the original drunken poet. So that was a kind of original take I had on poetry from him.

"A year later he invited me to come to his first seminary, which was a three-month retreat where we would alternate periods of teaching with periods of sitting for eight hours a day, doing *shamatha/vipassana* meditation, plain sitting and watching the breath. By 1972, he'd already given me some private meditation practice that involved some visualization and a special mantra, but at seminary he got everybody on one level with *shamatha*—plain sitting with mindfulness of the breathing. I went to several of these three-month retreats over the years.

"I began to do a lot of singing and writing, and he liked it. I did a song called 'Guru Blues' that went, 'I can't find anyone to tell me what to do / Can't find anyone, it's making me so blue / That I can't find anyone, anyone but

you / No, I can't find anyone, that knows me good as you /
Can't find anyone, only you, guru.'

"Trungpa had all sorts of ideas of poetics that interested me, partly in the Shambhala tradition, such as the
notion of speech, or *sambhogakaya*, uniting heaven and
earth, as in the traditional Taoist view that the emperor
unites heaven and earth. That is, speech unites the impalpable heaven (mind, thoughts) with the physiological body
(breath). So the body provides the palpable breath, the
mind provides the impalpable thoughts, and the speech
unifies them.

"His phrase would be, speech synchronizes—
proper speech synchronizes body and mind. He saw
poetry as proclamation from the seat, from your seat or
from your zafu or from your throne or from your chair as
teacher, or from your chair as meditator or your chair as a
human being or a Vajrayana student. Poetry as unhesitat-
ing and doubtless proclamation. Proclamation of what?
Proclamation of the actual mind, manifesting your mind,
writing the mind, which goes back to Kerouac but also goes
back to Milarepa, goes back to Trungpa's original instructions—don't you trust your own mind? Why do you need
a piece of paper?

"So, writing could be seen as 'writing your mind.'
In other words, you don't have to make anything up, you
don't have to fabricate anything, you don't have to fix up
something to say, which causes writer's block. All you have
to do is tap into the immediate mind of the moment—what
are you thinking about?—and just note it down, or observe
your own mind, or observe what's vivid coming to mind.

"Where do you start? Well, with the chaos of your
mind. How do you do it? Just tap into it and write what's
there in minute, particular detail. For the purpose of re-
lieving your own paranoia and others', revealing yourself

and communicating to others, which is a blessing for other people if you can communicate and relieve their sense of isolation, confusion, bewilderment, and suffering by offering your own mind as a sample of what's palpable, visible, and whatever little you've learned.

"My music started getting more focused on explicitly Buddhist themes because I thought I could handle them in American terms, just like Trungpa could handle Buddhist themes in Americanese. So I was a little bold in that and I thought it would be fun to try out dharma songs, like 'Do the Meditation Rock,' which is sung to the tune of 'I Fought the Law and the Law Won.'

"It's easy to combine a Buddhist message with a blues or folk idiom, because after all, blues is the same thing as samsara, the suffering of the cycle of birth and death. In Yiddish they call it *tsures*, which is also roughly equivalent to blues and samsara. So I have a lot of blues songs that are related to dharmic notions. But the main thing is to be open and candid and transparent: whether it's about Buddhism or just everyday life, you can be naked mentally, and candid, frank. Whether or not the work is overtly Buddhist doesn't matter, Buddhism is just reality. So the work reflects my own take on reality, which seems to correspond somewhat with Buddhist views.

"In 1987, after Trungpa died, I met Gelek Rinpoche through Philip Glass. I didn't know Gelek, but I heard that he was a friend of Trungpa's, so when I was invited to play at a benefit for Gelek in Detroit, I was happy to go. When I got off the tarmac at the airport, Gelek was there, looking just like Trungpa used to look: big brown lump. The same kind of high, enticing voice. And I just fell in love with him. Gelek is a lot less formal than Trungpa and doesn't try to adopt a royal, kingly thing.

"Since then I've spent a lot of time with Gelek and played some benefits for his organization, Jewel Heart. When we go on Buddhist retreats, Philip Glass and I generally cook up some new duet. The last retreat we did 'Sunflower Sutra' and a long poem on the cremation of Chögyam Trungpa, and a poem called 'The Way to the World Is Love.' And we keep evolving different pieces for the Tibet House benefits, or for benefits for Gelek."

While lecturing at Naropa in 1974, in a discourse entitled "First Thought, Best Thought," Ginsberg expanded on Trungpa's teachings concerning the relationship between meditation and spontaneous creativity. He talked about his own experience as a meditator and a writer, although his statements apply equally to songwriting or any creative act. "I've lately come to think of poetry as the possibility of simply articulating the movement of the mind, in other words, observing your mind, remembering maybe one or two thoughts back and laying it out, so in that sense it's as easy as breathing, because all you're doing is listening to particulars, those particulars of what you were just thinking about. And in that respect it's very close to meditation. Meditation is good practice for poetry. In other words, it's not the opposite, it's not an enemy of poetry. It was formerly seen to be, occasionally, by various hung-up intellectuals who were afraid they'd be silent and would not be able to be poets then. But actually all it does is give you lots of space to recollect what's going on in your mind, so providing lots of material, lots of ammunition, lots of material to work with.

"So if you're practicing in the line of Gertrude Stein and Kerouac, spontaneous transcription, transmission of your thought, how do you choose then what thoughts to put down? The answer is you don't get a chance to choose because everything's going so fast. So it's like driving on a road; you just have to follow the road and take the turns, eyeball it, as a carpenter would say. You don't have any scientific measuring rod, except your own mind, really, so you just have to chance wherever you can and pick whatever you can. So there's a process of automatic selection. Whatever you can draw into your net is it, what you got—whatever you can remember, and whatever you can manage physically to write down, is your poem. And you've got to trust that, as the principle of selection, so you have to be a little athletic about it, in the sense of developing means of transcription, ease of transcription, overcoming resistance to transcription."

In part, Ginsberg may have been reacting to criticism of the Beatnik writers as being unselective, but he was also presenting a radical idea: that the craft or technique of creating could be set aside and the artist function purely as a transcriber or conduit for unmediated inspiration, which is nothing other than direct perception of reality itself. Ginsberg's emphasis on the physical act of writing quickly suggests a deeper philosophical theme: trusting the inherent aesthetic perfection of one's first thought. Trungpa told him, "If the mind is shapely, the art will be shapely," and while working on a spontaneous chain poem together, the two came up with the Buddhist poetic formulation "first thought is best thought." Later, while lecturing at Naropa, Ginsberg elucidated the idea: "If you stick with first flashes, then you're all right. But the problem is, how do you get to that first thought—that's always the problem. The first thought is always the great elevated, cosmic, non-cosmic, *shunyata* thought. And then, at least according to the Buddhist formulation, after that you begin imposing names and forms and all that. So it's a question of catching yourself at your first open thought."

During a lecture given in Vienna in 1994, Ginsberg,

paraphrasing Trungpa, said, "Magic is the total delight in accident, the total pleasure in surprise mind, the appreciation of the fact that the mind changes, that one perception leads to another, and that in itself is a great play of mind. You don't have to go further in order to create a work of art."

Through *shamatha* meditation, he labored to generate mindfulness of the "first thought/best thought" and develop his ability to write poems and music based on direct perceptions. In *Meditation and Poetics*, Ginsberg went so far as to argue that poetry and mindfulness were inextricably linked. "Real poetry practitioners are practitioners of mind awareness, or practitioners of reality, expressing their fascination with a phenomenal universe and trying to penetrate to the heart of it." Later, referring to Burroughs and Kerouac alongside Ezra Pound and William Carlos Williams, Ginsberg writes, "The motive has been purification of mind and speech.

"You need a certain deconditioning of attitude—a deconditioning of rigidity and unyieldingness—so that you can get to the heart of your own thought. That's parallel with traditional Buddhist ideas of renunciation—renunciation of hand-me-down conditioned perceptions of mind. It's the meditative practice of 'letting go' of thoughts—neither pushing them away nor inviting them in, but, as you sit meditating, watching the procession of thought forms pass by, rising, flowering, and dissolving, and disowning them so to speak: you're not responsible any more than you're responsible for the weather, because you can't tell in advance what you're going to think next.

"So it requires cultivation of tolerance toward one's own thoughts and impulses and ideas—the tolerance necessary for the perception of one's own mind, the kindness to the self necessary for acceptance of that process of consciousness and for acceptance of the mind's raw contents, as in Walt Whitman's 'Song of Myself,' so that you can look from the outside into the skull and see what's there in your head."

Writing poetry and songs became a form of meditation for Ginsberg, in the sense that "vividness is self-selecting," meaning that keeping the mind loose, and allowing it to notice what it notices, defines both poetry and meditation. Under the guidance of Gelek Rinpoche, he also began to see a connection between poetry and bodhisattva activity, a connection between proclaiming the truth and actions motivated by perfect altruism toward all others. "There is a bodhisattva aspect of poetry, particularly when you combine it with the notion of poetry as proclamation. So, proclamation of original mind, proclamation of primordial mind, proclamation of your candid mind, proclamation of your own chaos, proclamation of your own uncertainty, proclamation of your own fragility, proclamation of your sensitivity, proclamation of your own cheerful neurosis, so to speak, a cheerful attitude toward your nature, which fits in well with the meditation practice suggestion in regular concentration on the breath; to take a friendly attitude toward your thoughts rather than trying to push them away or 'invite them in to tea,' merely observe them with a friendly attitude. And that can be applied to poetics, taking a friendly attitude toward your thoughts, and when you catch yourself thinking, if you have an interesting and vivid thought, noting it, particularly the sequence of thoughts that might lead other people to notice their own mind.

"In other words, if you can show your mind, it reminds people that *they* have a mind. If you can catch yourself thinking, it reminds people that they can catch *them*selves thinking. If you have a vivid moment that's more open and compassionate, it reminds people that *they* have those vivid moments.

"So by showing your mind as a mirror, you can make a mirror for other people to recognize their own minds and see familiarity and not feel that their minds are unworthy of affection or appreciation. Basically, poetics is appreciation of consciousness, appreciation of our own consciousness.

"Meditators have a slogan that says, 'Renunciation is a way to avoid conditioned mind.' That means that meditation is practiced by constantly 'renouncing' your thoughts, or 'letting go' of your thoughts. That doesn't mean letting go of your whole awareness—only that small part of your mind that's dependent on linear, logical thinking. It doesn't mean renouncing intellect, which has its proper place in Buddhism, as it does in Blake. It doesn't mean idiot wildness. It means expanding the area of awareness so that your awareness surrounds your thoughts, rather than that you enter into your thoughts like a dream. Thus the life of meditation and the life of art are both based on a similar conception of spontaneous mind. They both share renunciation as a way of avoiding a conditioned art work, or trite art, or repetition of other people's ideas."

Despite his extensive experience with meditation and introspective nature, Ginsberg's work as a poet and musician was always political, and at times revolutionary in its intent. Although he became a highly respected man of letters, in the rigidly conservative mileu of America in the 1950s and early 1960s, his open homosexuality and scathing criticism of the military-industrial complex made him a threatening figure to the status quo, and his critiques of big business and the American military establishment continued to his death. At the 1996 benefit for Tibet House,

Ginsberg sang a song called "The Ballad of the Skeletons," which he had first played at a benefit for death-row prisoner Mumia Abu-Jamal. The song excoriates both American corporate greed and the world's attempt to ignore the Chinese oppression of Tibet.

"The Ballad of the Skeletons" was Ginsberg's last recording. "We recorded it with David Mansfield, Marc Ribot, and Lenny Kaye, and we shipped the tape to Paul McCartney and he added maracas and drums and organ and guitar and gave it a dramatic shape, responding to the voice. And then Philip Glass added piano arpeggios, so that completed my band, and then Hal Wilner mixed it. So it was really like sangha working together."

In a 1982 interview with James MacKenzie, Ginsberg places his most famous poem, *Howl*, in the context of the historical "vocalization of the poem," a process at whose center he placed Dylan, but in which he also rightly saw himself as occupying a central role. "With *Howl* it was from voice to spoken conversation voice to chant, or to long-breath chant, tending in the bardic-chanting direction, the ecstatic direction, and then from chanting it actually moves to song with Dylan in the next generation: and so returns to us as song. Now I am in an interesting situation where a lot of material I do, write, compose, the only extant manuscripts are chance tape recordings of poetry readings I improvise. So at almost every poetry reading I do some improvisation, you know, at one point or another—sometimes extended, sometimes generally rhymed blues form or ballad form, and I'm just slowly verging toward trying to improvise without music, you know, and trying to do my regular forms like *Howl* or 'Sunflower' or something like that, without the crutch of music, or rhyme."

When Ginsberg, then seventy, cast a long eye back

on his career as a musician and spiritual seeker, he saw four distinct phases: his early experimentation with sacred music, the Blake recordings, the Dylan-influenced folk era, and most recently, what he called his politicized rock and roll. "The first exposure I had to formal Buddhist practice was in 1963 in India, where I heard Gary Snyder chanting the *Prajnaparamita-sutra*. Then I got Suzuki Roshi's permission to chant it to a tune of my own, and later I worked on that with Gelek, tinkering with the translation. So I moved from what I call sacred music, the chanting of mantras and sutras, to Blake—which is also sacred music—to seeing everyday folk music and even rock and roll as a vehicle for sacred expression, and then finally merging with this sort of political rock and roll, with a little help from my friends."

Despite the close relationship that Ginsberg enjoyed with Trungpa and other teachers, he never became a regular meditator. But his devotion to the practice was evident, and in his own way, he developed a successful practice. "I'm not a very good meditator, I must say. I'm a flaky Buddhist. I feel that I should be doing more and now that I'm retiring from Brooklyn College, I hope to rest a little bit more and spend more time at home."

Author's Note: Allen Ginsberg passed away on April 5, 1997, a few months after this interview was conducted.

JEFF BUCKLEY
Knowing Not Knowing

JEFF BUCKLEY

Early in the spring of 1997, singer and songwriter Jeff Buckley headed down to Memphis to begin pre-production on what would have been his second full-length album. A few weeks after Buckley arrived, his bandmates flew in from New York to join him. He was in high spirits: the songwriting was going well, and he was reunited with his group. The same night his band arrived Buckley went out for a late-night stroll to a Memphis harbor and waded into the river. He had always admired Led Zeppelin, and was singing "Whole Lotta Love" when a boat passed in front of him. He lost his footing, perhaps dragged into the water by the boat's wake, and was never seen alive again. He was thirty years old, two years older than his father, the folksinger Tim Buckley, had been when he died of a drug overdose.

I first met Jeff Buckley and saw him perform about two years before he passed away. It was near midnight and Buckley was sitting in the back office of a Tower Records store in lower Manhattan. Buckley had become a scion of the Lower East Side antifolk scene, and was preparing for an in-store performance in support of his album *Grace*.

But first he needed to do something: he insisted on listening to a crackly old recording of "The Man That Got Away" by Judy Garland, on the pretext that he wanted the store manager, who had given the CD to Buckley, to understand how magnificent a gift it was. Buckley needed to demonstrate the album's beauty. He had also picked up gratis CD reissues of vintage Aretha Franklin and Nina Simone records, and two albums by Nusrat Fateh Ali Khan, who had a major influence on Buckley's singing. While Buckley could occasionally summon the same kind of ecstatic vocal power that was Khan's trademark, his singing had more in common with Garland's delicate, vulnerable warble.

Buckley was an unglamorous star. That night he was wearing a wretched pair of weathered combat boots—the sort you occasionally see homeless men selling—a frumpy gray cardigan sweater, and jeans that hadn't been washed in a long time. Ditto his hair. In an oddly white-trash bit of accessorizing, Buckley's wallet was attached to his belt by a chain, in the style favored by motorcycle gangs. Three days of beard growth rounded out his anti-coif, but his sex appeal remained intact: a nervous girl approached to ask if, as she suspected, he was a Scorpio. Another pressed a poem she had written for him into his hand. He folded it carefully and put it in his pocket, as though he would cherish it forever. Maybe he did.

Buckley was at an odd moment in his career when he died. Having moved to New York several years before from California, where he was raised by his mother, he crawled his way up through the ranks of the insular lower Manhattan music scene. He had become a mini-star in that highly circumscribed microcosm, perched on the cusp of national and international success. That night at Tower Records the line between Lower East Side local hero and international stardom seemed pretty thin. On one hand, his debut album sold several hundred thousand copies (although more in Europe than in America), and there was a throng of photographers and autograph-seekers pressing

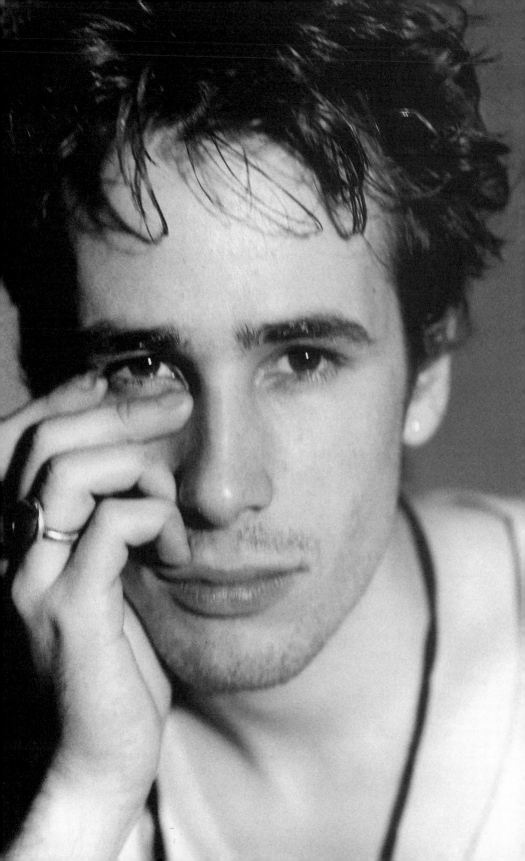

around him. On the other hand, he wasn't above hauling his own gear onstage, more or less indistinguishable from the half dozen stringy-haired sound men and roadies who were putting the sound system in place.

Buckley had no video in heavy rotation on MTV, largely because he insisted that people judge the music on the way it sounded before supplying them with an accompanying image. For the same reason, he refused to even suggest a single to radio deejays. "What I'd love," Buckley said, "is if a deejay had a lineup of songs, and he'd just use one of my songs as part of a really nice evening. But that's the way I would deejay, not the way they do it. They usually have playlists."

For a guy with folksinging in his blood, Buckley had assembled an arsenal of prog-rock guitar effects you'd expect at an Emerson, Lake, and Palmer show and had set his amp at cat-spaying volume. (In fact, he had been raised on Led Zeppelin and Kiss.) Several dozen more stringy-haired people with assorted rings in their lips and noses (his fans) materialized. As he stepped onto the makeshift stage, a grumpy security guard began clearing some fans from a stairway, but Buckley interjected: "Wait! Those are my friends! Can they stay there? I give them special permission." What started as dispensation for four friends ended up being extended to anybody who wanted to stay.

The set began with a ghostly wail from Buckley, and a mildly Middle Eastern guitar line. He sang with a vibrato that quivered like the tongue of a snake. It was so atmospheric that you hardly realized his bandmates were rocking their tits off. That was the tension: Buckley ululating in sensual falsetto, the band churning out mid-seventies Led Zep knockoffs. He seemed a strangely ethereal cherub in the midst of all that visceral thrash.

After the show, Buckley signed autographs, taking

several minutes with the thirty or so fans who lined up for an audience with the tousle-haired singer. Rather than just scribbling an autograph, he wrote a personal note to each person. Everything he did seemed to place poetry before commerce, but I couldn't help wondering if it was all an elaborate ruse, a crafty stance aimed at those disenchanted with the slickness of pop posturing. Didn't Buckley, after all, want to make a lot of money and sell records?

"If it happens it'd be great," he said later that night, over omelettes and wine at an all-night eatery, "but we just play to express. I want to live my life playing music, so that we can be immersed in it. In order to learn how deep it goes, you have to be in it."

As to why he took so much time with each of the fans who asked for an autograph, Buckley articulated his basic anti-rock-star stance: "The way I experience a performance is that there's an exchange going on. It's not just my ego being fed. It's thoughts and feelings. Raw expression has its own knowledge and wisdom." He trailed off, as though humbled by the mere thought of his audience wanting to hear him play, or asking him for an autograph. "I've been in their position before and all I wanted was to show my appreciation to the performer. So I feel like it's kind of generous of them to even be asking me for an autograph.

"It's true that there's also the people who want a piece of you," he conceded. "But it's pretty hard to keep feeling protective all the time, because there's really nothing to protect yourself against. Sometimes people shout at me on the street, and they feel they know me through my music. But that doesn't substitute for a real personal relationship. I don't feel like people know me, I just think we share a love for music in common, and for some reason they key into the way I play. I feel appreciative when people come up to me, and I feel good when we connect. Usually, it serves as a nice comedown after a performance. Any other conduct would bust the groove, because I'm buzzing when I get offstage, and I'm consciously protecting that connection because that's what got me through the performance in the first place. It's an invocation and worship of this certain feeling, this direct line to your heart, and somehow music does that more powerfully than anything else. It's like a total, immediate elixir."

By all appearances Buckley conformed to the stereotype of the poetic artist: largely lacking the practical, thick-skinned psychic barrier that separates most of us from the harsh realities of life. With a rabbit-like nervous disposition and a hypersensitive vulnerability that bordered on tragicomic, he looked like he was about to burst into tears at any moment. His face was contorted and slightly tortured-looking during most of the interview, though I got the impression that it wasn't so much the experience of being interviewed that was torturing him but the pain of grappling with his own thoughts and the world around him.

Relationships were at the heart of Buckley's world. Although he was marketed as a solo artist, the attitude he had toward his listeners mirrored the relationship he formed with his three-piece backing band. "Playing with a band is all about accepting a bond, accepting everything the way it is. It takes a lot of patience and a lot of taking chances with each other. It takes seeing each other in weak and strong lights, and accepting both, and utilizing the high and low points of your relationship."

It wasn't only interpersonal relationships that Buckley held sacred—he was aware of making his music in relation to all the sounds around him. The environment was Buckley's co-composer: to his ears, no melody or rhythm was separate from the sounds going on in the background. "It's not like music begins or ends. All kinds of sounds are working into each other. Sometimes I'll just stop on the street because there's a sequence of sirens going on; it's like a melody I'll never hear again. In performance, things can be meaningful or frivolous, but either way the musical experience is totally spontaneous, and new life comes out of it, meaning if you're open to hearing the way music interacts with ambient sound, performance never feels like a rote experience. It's pretty special sometimes, the way a song affects a room, the way you're in complete rhythm with the song. When you're emotionally overcome, and there's no filter between what you say and what you mean, your language becomes guttural, simple, emotional, and full of pictures and clarity. Were you to transcribe it, it might not make sense, but music is a totally different language."

"People talk all day in a practical way, but real language that penetrates and affects people and carries wisdom is something different. Maybe it's the middle of the afternoon and you see a child's moon up in the sky, and you feel like it's such a simple, pure, wonderful thing to look at. It just hits you in a certain way, and you point it out to a stranger, and he looks at you like you're weird and walks away. To speak that way, to point out a child's moon to a stranger, is original language, it's the way you originate yourself. And the cool thing is, if you catch people in the right moment, it's totally clear. Without knowing why, it's simply clear. That sort of connection is very empirical. It comes from the part of you that just understands immediately. All these types of things are gold, and yet they are dishonored or not paid attention to because that kind of tender communication is so alien in our culture, *except* in performance. There's a wall up between people all day long, but performance transcends that convention. If pop music were really seen as a fine art or if fine art were popular, I don't know what the hell would happen—this wouldn't be the same country, because if the masses of people began to respect and really open to fine art, it would bring about a huge shift in consciousness.

"Music is so many things. It's not just the performer. It's the audience and the architecture of the song, and each builds off the other. Music is a setting for poignancy, anger, destruction, total disaster, total wrongness, and then—like a little speck of gold in the middle of it—excitement, but excitement in a way that matters. Excitement that is not just aesthetically pleasing but shoots some sort of understanding into you."

Buckley's songs were composed with made-up chords, bright harmonic clusters that seem too obvious not to have been written before, yet they rarely feel formulaic. There's a lot of open strumming, suggesting that the songs were written largely for the sheer physical pleasure of playing them. He and his band modified the arrangements during each performance, playing with an elasticity and openness typical of Buckley's personality. "Hearing a song is like meeting somebody. A song is something that took time to grow and once it's there, it's on its own. Every time you perform it, it's different. It has its own structure, and you have to flow through it, and it has to come through you."

Buckley's entire career reflected his outsider's approach to the music business. When he arrived in New York, rather than recording a demo or finding an agent, he simply began to perform for free. He played at a small café on the Lower East Side of Manhattan, and before long, crowds were lined up out the door. As a result, representatives of record companies sought out Buckley, rather than the other way around. "There is a distinct separation of sensibility between art as commerce and art as a way of life. If you buy into one too heavily it eats up the other. If instead of having songs happen as your life happens, you're getting a song together because you need a certain number of songs on a release to be sold, the juice is sucked out immediately. That approach kills it."

Still, it took a strong belief in one's art to sit in a small café and trust that the world's record companies would come calling. Buckley played down his seemingly effortless approach to career as though it were common-sense. "I just wanted to learn certain things. I wanted to just explore, like a kid with crayons. It took a while for me to get a record contract, but it also took a tremendous amount of time for me to feel comfortable playing, and that's all I was concerned with. And I'm still concerned with that, mainly.

"I don't think about my responsibility as a musician in terms of any kind of religious significance. I don't have any allegiance to an organized religion; I have an alle-giance to the gifts that I find for myself in those religions. They seem to be saying the same thing, they just have dif-ferent mythologies and expressions, but the dogma of reli-gions and the way they're misused is all too much of a trap. I'd rather be nondenominational, except for music. I pre-fer to learn everything through music. If you want divinity, the music in every human being and their love for music is pretty much it. It's the big indication of their spirituality and their ability to love and make love, or feel pain or joy, and really manifest it, really be real. But I don't believe in a big guy with a beard on a throne, telling us that we're bad; I certainly don't believe in original sin. I believe in the opposite of that: you have an Eden immediately from the time you are born, but as you are conditioned by your caretakers and your surroundings, you may lose that original thing. Your task is to get back to it, so you can claim responsibility for your own perfection."

Buckley considered the development of awareness to be the main goal of his life. "I think of it as trying to get more aligned with the feeling of purity in music, however it sounds. I think music is prayer. Sometimes people make up prayers and they don't even know it. They just make up a song that has rhyme and meter, and once it's made, it can carry on a life of its own. It can have a lot of juice to it and a lot of meaning: there's no end to the different individual flavors that people can bring to the musical form.

"In order to make the music actual, you have to enable it to be. And that takes facing some things inside you that constrict you, your own impurity and mistakes and blockages. As you open up yourself, the music opens up in different directions that lead you in yet other directions."

Asking most pop musicians if they're satisfied with record sales is like asking models about the aging process: they say they don't care, but it's hard to believe. For commercial recording artists, sales are the only objective indicator of whether they're doing things right—that fans are sincerely motivated to walk into record stores by the tens or by the millions, pull out their wallets, and pay for the music. But with his quiet, unaffected voice nearly a whisper, Buckley steadfastly maintained that he really didn't want to sell a million records—and it was strangely believable. When he talked about multiplatinum-selling bands who felt "disappointed" by a mere five million copies sold, the disgust he felt for commercialism was palpable. "The only valuable thing about selling records, the only thing that matters, is that people connect and that you keep on growing. You do make choices based on how many people you reach, meaning, now that I have a relationship with strangers worldwide, I have to try not to let it become too much of a factor and just accept it. The limited success we've had in the past is definitely a factor, it's just there. It just is. The whole thing is such a crapshoot, you can't really control what your appeal is gonna be. My music ain't gonna make it into the malls, but it doesn't matter. I don't really care to make it into the malls.

"Whether I sell a lot of records or not isn't up to me. You can sell a lot of records, but that's just a number sold—that's not understood, or loved, or cherished.

"Take someone like Michael Jackson. Early on he sacrificed himself to his need to be loved by all. His talent and his power were so great that he got what he wanted but he also got a direct, negative result, which is that he's not able to grow into an adult human being. And that's why his music sounds sort of empty and weird.

"Being the kind of person I am, fame is really over-whelming. First of all, just being faced with the questions that everybody faces: Do I matter? Should I go on? Why am I here? Is this really that important? All that low self-esteem shit. You're constantly trying to make sure that your sense of self-worth doesn't depend on the writings or opinions of other people. You have to wean yourself off acclaim as the object of your work, by learning to depend on your own judgment and knowing what it is that you enjoy. You have to realize what the difference is between being adored and being loved and understood. Big difference.

"I don't really have super-pointed answers to the big questions. I'm in the middle of a mystery myself. I'm not even that developed at having a real psycho-religious epistemology about what I feel. All I can tell you is that I feel. It's just the same old fight to constantly be aware. It's an ongoing thing. It'll never be a static perfect thing or a static mediocre thing, it just has its rise and fall."

DEAD CAN DANCE

The Sacred Tongue

Lisa Gerrard speaks carefully. Her words fall out in complete phrases, like stones that have been carried around for a long time in somebody's hands until they are rubbed smooth. Gerrard, who is the lead singer for the ambient world music duo Dead Can Dance, is painstaking and poetic in her efforts to explain her music and its spiritual significance. At times she is so poetic that you begin to wonder if she is making sense at all. But Gerrard does makes sense, musically and philosophically. With her partner, Brendan Perry, she has recorded seven albums as part of Dead Can Dance, and one, *The Mirror Pool*, as a solo artist. Perhaps the only unifying element in the wide-ranging Dead Can Dance oeuvre is an unearthly, ghostly quality, a sense that cyclical time is in effect and ancient rhythms and words are restored and breathing anew. Indeed, the name of the band is a reference to aboriginal masks carved from dead or dying trees, thereby giving them new life.

Although Dead Can Dance have, over their sixteen-year career, consistently refused to take part in the usual career-boosting activities, such as music videos and large-scale tours, their recent album *Spiritchaser* nonetheless topped *Billboard* magazine's world music charts. Perry and Gerrard are both of Anglo-Irish descent and their domination of a genre normally associated with artists from Africa,

South America, and Asia calls into question the very definition of *world music*. With their richly layered polyrhythms and exquisite blending of aboriginal, Celtic, African, and otherworldly melodies, Dead Can Dance make music that is at once entrancing, primal, and exploratory. It is panethnic without sounding self-consciously multicultural. Dead Can Dance seem to be digging for the collective voice of humanity, searching for the rhythms and melodies that bind indigenous musical forms from all around the world.

When Gerrard talks about her music, she always refers to it as "the work," an indication of the seriousness with which she makes music. In the wake of her brother's death last year, she experienced firsthand the way that music could provide transcendent connections.

"I don't think of the work connecting with physical relationships in everyday life," Gerrard says. "I see it as something of an aftermath of physical relationships. For example, shortly after I lost my brother Mark, I came home and I listened to *The Mirror Pool* with his wife. Up until that time, I'd never understood that particular piece of work and I felt quite concerned about it, because I was beginning to worry that my musicality had become fragmented. It was as though someone had thrown a plate up in the air and it had broken into pieces on the ground and each fragment was a voice that I was singing through. And I thought, is it that I'm not whole within the work, is it that somehow cracks are showing?

"I now see a completely different scenario since I brought my sister-in-law home and she said, 'Let me hear your new work.' We were both very grieved at the loss of my brother and suddenly, when listening to the work, we experienced it as a chariot to carry his soul into the afterlife. There was a wonderful reality that took place for me because I no longer saw the fragments but saw the whole as an external experience. And not only did I see myself witnessing the whole, but I saw the being that saw myself witnessing the whole.

"Because of a death or a loss or something that happens in our lives, all of a sudden it becomes clear to us what this work is about at that moment. Then we stand back from the being that is making that analysis and, with another part of our being, are able to see the being that's making that analysis function. And we can continually step back and have greater perspective. So we can look at the fractures within the human constitution; by understanding our work it becomes a mirror into the very complex architecture of the person. This is what's so interesting about music: it allows both the composer and the listener to enter rooms that are part of the human psyche they normally wouldn't enter."

Gerrard believes music has the potential to integrate people's minds and bodies, to strengthen faith, to serve as a sort of workout for the soul. In that regard, she maintains that it is impossible to judge music as successful or as good or bad. Instead she speaks of "musical maturation," in which the potential of music to touch the soul directly is more effectively realized. Reflecting further on the transcendent moment when she and her sister-in-law grieved her brother's loss, she no longer ascribes the experience to the music but rather to her emotional state as a listener. "I could listen to that same piece of work today and it would sound like the work of a fractured child. I could stand back and look at this work objectively without a very powerful experience like grief looming over me and see exactly where I stood in my artisanship when I wrote it. So the work that we do is subjective—it's relative to where we stand today as listeners, and not only as composers.

"It's possible to look at the work and see it becoming more mature or less mature as the result of your experiences. Because of your experience of loss and your heart being put into a different place—maybe a better place—you are able to see more clearly the process of creativity, to see the bridge that you're trying to make for your soul to travel on its journey through your life experience. What is soul? Soul is that which we don't see; we only know it's there through our ability to have faith."

Because Gerrard is dealing with such ephemeral and personal issues, collaborating radically changes the sound of her music. The Dead Can Dance partnership, she says, is essential to making her work palatable to a larger audience. "When I work with Brendan, I'm a guilded laborer. When I work by myself, I'm a collector of dreams. When I work alone, I don't have to compromise, I don't have to prepare, I don't have to compare notes, I don't have to be guided through this labyrinth of reality.

"Whereas with Brendan, the work that we do is so architectural. What do we rely on to bring us into deep contact with harmony? In the physical world, we rely on architecture, on synchronicity, and on symmetrical forms. We rely on things being in harmony to the visual eye. In the realm of music, we look for that same symmetry and balance. That's the only level on which we can really judge music as good or bad: on the level of its architecture.

"The other dimension that we're allowed to experience is something much more personal, and we make a choice as to whether we're going to surrender ourselves or not. That's why people say, 'Oh, your work is spiritual, I don't understand it.' Why is our work 'spiritual' and another composer's not? People say that there is soul in our work, but why do they hear soul in one work and not in another? What is soul in music? Soul is that which we cannot see but which through our faith we give life to. So we start to unravel this essential property that exists within humans that leads us into the abstract world. When somebody says there is soul in the work, it means that through the music they have allowed themselves to unlock doors within their own unconscious, that through their confidence—I used the word *faith* before, but let's not confuse this with religiosity—through their confidence, they have allowed themselves to surrender, so that they can look inside.

"It's not possible for me to release the work I do alone, because of people's need for architecture and symmetry. This is my private language, it's where I go and explore my sacred tongue. My solo album was an attempt to create architecture as the chariot for my sacred tongue, but it didn't really work very well. I was trying to create something to allow those sacred tongues to live in some sort of scenario, because I'm trying to bridge two realities: architecture and essence."

Striking a balance between craft and instinct is, of course, a common problem for artists, but the search for that balance is particularly crucial in Dead Can Dance's approach to making music. Gerrard has spoken of trying to find "the abstract vocabulary of the collective unconscious." Recording in several non-English languages—as well as in made-up words—she has long sought to discover a way of singing that would communicate with listeners regardless of the language they spoke.

"To me language gets in the way of communicating. I mean, I could convey to you in six seconds what I feel my work is about if I could communicate with you telepathically. Instead, we're going down this clumsy, awkward road, trying to explain things that really should not be explained. In a way, trying to explain is forbidden; you do it and it puts holes in your energy. But at the same time, we need to make an effort to explain, as long as we stay true to what we feel. But it can be extremely traumatic, because you see the whole, and you see this finger pointing toward some form of perfection, and it brings you into the reality of how imperfect we are as human beings. To get stuck in that ping-pong between realities is very traumatic."

Gerrard feels that successful music is made in two ways—in what she calls the internal or abstract, the spontaneous outpourings, and in what she calls the external or architectural, meaning the song structures that adhere in some way to pop conventions. "In the external, of course, there is commercially successful music being made. But in the internal, the most successful music you make is unlistenable to the other person. It's the sort of work that, if you heard someone call it pretty, you'd jump them. You're too close to it to hear it called pretty or nice. It's too disappointing. We need to go slowly: in order to communicate and rebuild the language, it's going to take an entire lifetime. And the language is going to have to be rebuilt within the architectural structure that exists around these sacred languages. Because that's how to present them, in a way that people can *kind* of understand, so it's not so wacky and off-the-wall.

"It's like death and birth and the journey between the two. I know that my musical tongue was the tongue that I had before I was born. And I'm hoping that tongue won't be unfamiliar to me at the moment when I leave my physical body. The worst scenario for me at the moment of death would be fear, the opposite of love. Fear is the very state which we mustn't be in when we leave the physical body. We need to collect our confidence by uncovering these unconscious languages and our feelings that are conveyed through the abstract, so that when all that we have left is our abstract, we are familiar with it."

Throughout all twists and turns of their career, undoubtedly the greatest threat to the existence of Dead Can Dance came in 1987, when Gerrard and Perry broke off their five-year romance. That they were able to continue as a professional entity, and maintain a warm personal relationship even after Gerrard got married, is testimony to the depth of their musical bond.

"I think the only reason we were together in the first place was because of our musical empathy. Our work was our first love. When we met, we were both performing as separate artists and had absolutely no intention of working together at all. The things that I was doing were appalling to Brendan—they were too abstract and too weird, and too 'avant-garde,' he called them. That was the first time I'd ever heard that word, *avant-garde*, because I was only sixteen at the time, and I ran around trying to find out what the hell it meant. Then we did a piece of music together quite by accident, after being close friends for about three years, and we found that something really magical happened when we worked together. All of the practical qualities that I lacked existed in the work that Brendan did, and all of the delicate abstracts that were lacking in his work existed in mine. When we worked together something took place that we couldn't possibly have done alone."

For a brief period of time after Gerrard and Perry broke off their romantic relationship, they collaborated from a distance. He would concoct rhythms and music tracks in his studio in Ireland, and mail tapes of the works in progress to Gerrard, who would record vocal tracks half a world away in Australia.

"We worked separately after working together on a

film in Spain, during which we pushed our creative relationship to its absolute limit. Drinking a bottle of whiskey
a day and smoking sixty cigarettes a day . . . it bruised us
spiritually and it bruised our relationship. We needed to
get away from each other after that and we thought it was
the end. Then about a year later I rang him and said, 'We
need to work together,' and he said, 'You're absolutely
right, we're insane, I can't cope without you.' And I said,
'Well, I can't cope without you. There's still more work that
we haven't done. We can always work with other artists,
but there's something very important that we have yet to
do.' It wasn't that we couldn't cope without each other musically—in some ways we do a lot better musically without
each other—it's that there's still something that we need to
learn from each other.

"Just before I went to Ireland to work with Brendan
again, I received a very sacred tongue, a prayer tongue. I
suddenly realized that what I thought of as the spiritual
attributes of my work were something separate from this
other, automatic language, which could never be recorded
because it lived in a perfect world and could never be cap-
tured. So I was no longer trying to use the work to repair
this terrible accident that happened at the beginning of
time."

What Gerrard refers to as the sacred tongue is a
pure musical form not at all concerned with "architecture." She arrives at her music through a highly personal
process, yet the practicalities of the business side of her life
seem rarely to impinge on the quest for what is sacred.

"The work is not only my way of understanding
who I am and why we're all here, but it also helps me keep
a roof over my family's head. All of these things are inter-
linked, and there is a practical side to the work. If I give
up this work, can I expect to be maintained by the state as

a priestess to explore these things? It doesn't work that way. I have to earn money. The thing with the work is that I won't arrive at an ideal world and I'm aware of that, but I hope to structure a language through which I can communicate with others.

"It's really hard for me to explain; but I don't sing with words because I can't communicate what I want to communicate with words. I know what takes place during the dance of creating work, and it's possible for me to see my gate, my doorways, that give me contact with myself as a whole. I have contact with a much larger body, this is the thing that makes the work sacred, and other people come into contact with those realities. I'm sure it's not gonna happen just by someone putting a CD on their stereo—maybe a touch of it—but these are things that are communicated for a community that embraces these things together. It happens in live performances.

"The power of music is the power to connect with the abstract, and we dare to exploit this. It's really important that young people are allowed to find music free from the seductions of marketing, and be able to make a conscious choice. That's why we've always kept a low profile: because we want to be sure that when people come to our shows, they're there because they chose by themselves to be there."

It is for this reason that Dead Can Dance avoid creating music videos that might attract casual listeners to their performances. Gerrard says that she would prefer to sell fewer records and play to fewer people, provided her audiences were composed entirely of die-hard fans. "I want them to have to look under stones to find us. I want us to come into their lives like an accident. When we were young there were many opportunities to take a great big advance and go off and work for two years and that would be the end of it. That's not what this is about for us. This is about people being able to come together and embrace something that centers them."

AL GREEN
Making a Joyful Sound

The first time I saw Al Green in person I was in Memphis to hear a southern rock band whose name I can't remember anymore. One Sunday morning, between forays to the city's barbecue joints and innocently hedonistic music industry dinners (the band gets drunk, the writers get drunk, the local deejay gets into a food fight with the band, and so on), I decided to take a cab out to the Reverend Mr. Green's church.

It wasn't until later that I found out how silly it was to assume Green would actually be at his church. Apparently, it was rare to find the Reverend presiding over services because most Sundays he was traveling, performing, or otherwise occupied by his music career. But this Sunday, Green was ministering in full effect, decked out in purple robes, sweating like a wild man in the Memphis summertime. With tourists seated next to us from as far away as Germany and Africa, we were treated to a full-on southern Baptist gospel performance—and not only by the Reverend Mr. Green but by Al Green the soul singer.

There are people today who grew up in black Baptist churches who remember deacons who could discern, simply by looking at the way your body moved to the music, whether you were taken by the spirit of Jesus or you were dancing sinfully to the music of the devil. While some of those old-school Southern Baptist deacons would tan

your hide for hearing gospel the wrong way, that morning in Memphis, Al Green made it clear that what makes soul music work in nightclubs is the same thing that makes gospel work in church. As he explained, it's all one music, with one message of love. He said that when he first became a man of the cloth, he assumed he'd have to stop singing the secular soul music that had made him a wealthy celebrity by the early 1970s. But he took a careful listen to those songs, he said, and realized there was no divide between the message of his secular love songs and the message of the Bible. With that, he launched into "Let's Stay Together," followed by "Love and Happiness"—short, emotional songs that grooved along as the church band tapped out the rhythms amid the fluttering of fans from the older female parishioners and the occasional Amen! issuing forth from the pews.

I didn't get the chance to speak with Al Green until several years later, when we sat down in a black marble-and-mirrors-type corporate conference room in his record company's mid-Manhattan offices. The Reverend was dressed in something that looked like a Richard Simmons workout-wear adaptation of Jimi Hendrix's brocade jacket. His hair was in full coiffure. He had big flashy rings and big flashy eyes and big flashy teeth, all of which he used to dramatic effect during pauses in his conversation.

Green tends to smile knowingly, as though to signify that you already know what he's thinking and there's really no need to say it. To make matters more complex and entertaining, he tends to break into gleeful melodies in the middle of his sentences. Coupled with his conspiratorial style and occasionally impenetrable "logic," this can make an interview with Al Green something like a tango with a snake charmer. You're not sure if you're going to leave with everything you came in with.

The Reverend doesn't exactly chat; he sermonizes in a way that snowballs in intensity, volume, and exuberance. We began talking about the difference between secular love songs and love songs to God.

"The reason I sang songs like 'Everything Is Gonna Be Alright' and 'What the World Needs Now' after I became a reverend is because the message is love. Love is the message and the message is love, and I feel very good by saying that. A love you might feel for your wife or your neighbor or your companion is love in a sphere that you can relate to, because that's the sphere you live in. When you start talking about a higher love, which is the spiritual side of the holy tabernacle, which is what you saw in my church in Memphis—then you're talking about another element. Both of those elements deserve a great and wonderful applause because they come from the same great master. He put them both here: the love between the man and the woman, and the love between you and me, because 'you're mine, I made you, I can't abandon you.'

"The love between a man and his wife continues along a spectrum to a love for a higher power. It's an extension of the same kind of strength. When I'm writing music, I'm actually saying my prayers. I write my prayers down on the paper on my workbench, where I have my piano, and my clavinet, and my music paper. I'm really writing down my prayers. [Starts singing] 'Spending my day, thinkin 'bout you girl, hmmm' [laughs] That's a good prayer. When you write a song, you're the conduit, you're the vessel by which an idea is related."

While some Christian fundamentalists might argue that a song that describes thinking about a girl, rather than Jesus, is decidedly *not* a prayer, Green contends that you can sing about God in many ways and that scriptural literalists may be losing sight of the big picture. For Green, the decision to substitute *girl* for *Jesus* represents a conscious decision to balance the principles of the gospel with commercial interests. "See, I'm selling music. We already know the principles that my music is geared to, and when I sing, 'Spending my day, thinking about you girl,' that gives my music a greater outlet, makes it more available to people. It's more acceptable if you sing 'girl.' At first, I didn't know that, but now I'm putting the message in a language that everybody can understand. [Sings] 'Since I met Judy, ain't no love like my baby!' You can understand that. We use different pictures, but you know what the actual fact is, that which is eternal and cannot be seen. Because we've come to realize that the things that cannot be seen, they will last forever. The temporal things are gonna get old, disintegrate, disappear."

Self-importance is a pitfall all spiritual leaders face, especially when it is magnified by the preacher's role as quasi-performer. On the issue of egotism, Green suggests that he's grown humbler over the years. "An old blues artist who used to blow the harmonica and play the guitar on a street corner in Memphis told me, never take yourself too seriously. When I talk with someone like B. B. King, or Ray Charles, that's when I begin to come down off my high horse. They remind me that you should never become greater than the people you're interacting with. Keep it humble, don't be over everybody, don't be the head. I don't travel with a big entourage or bodyguards, none of that."

Al Green was born in Forrest City, Arkansas, in 1946 and moved to Grand Rapids, Michigan, at the age of nine. It was there that he formed his first act, a gospel group with his brothers, eventually shifting toward secular pop. (His father was said to have "fired" him from the group on one occasion for listening to the "profane" music of Jackie Wilson.) His career as a recording artist began in the early 1960s, when he started playing with a band called the Creations on what was known as the "chitlin' circuit," a string of juke joints in black communities across the Midwest and South, and recording for the Zodiac label.

Although he had a hit with a slowed-down version of the Temptations' "Can't Get Next to You" in 1971, it was not until early the next year that "Let's Stay Together" topped the charts, beginning a string of hits that continued through most of the decade. In 1973 his ex-girlfriend, Mary Woodson, fatally shot herself after scalding him with burning-hot grits. The next year Green became a reverend, which many writers have attributed to Woodson's death, although he maintains that the two events were not directly related.

"Her death was really tragic because she was a beautiful person who could share with you on a very deep level. A warm, understanding person, but she was really out of control at the time and I didn't know it. If I had known I would have made sure she had the medicine she needed to keep her mind balanced."

The actual moment of Green's conversion to born-again Christianity, he says, took place during his sleep. He was in a Los Angeles hotel suite. "I had done two shows that night, one show at the Cow Palace and one at Disneyland. I said goodnight to my girlfriend, who was in the bedroom watching TV, and I was sleeping on a couch in an outer room. The next thing I knew, I was up at four-thirty in the morning, being changed and being translated and being atoned for. It's really more than I can talk about in an interview."

Green had been brought up in the church but he wasn't particularly religious, nor did he have any sense that he would one day be born again. "I was brought up in the church and everything was fine and dandy, but I had girlfriends, I liked to drink Champale, and I had a big entourage."

The conversion was one of those mythic lightning-bolt experiences. The morning after, he went home and entered what he describes as a trancelike state. "After that night in the hotel room, I was so caught up with what was going on, and what had happened to me was so stunning, that I didn't really come to my senses for six or seven days. I was kind of in a trance for a long time. There were all these weird things happening. Not long after, I was playing a gig at La Casino in Cherry Hill, New Jersey, and I was up onstage, singing 'You Oughta Be with Me,' tears coming down both cheeks. The band was cooking. Everybody stopped dancing and started looking at me with tears streaming down my face. As I was walking down the runway into the audience, I heard some guy say, 'Wow, this guy is really serious about this song he's singing, he's actually crying.' I was singing, 'You oughta be with me until I die' and everyone stopped dancing and they just began to clap and sing 'You oughta be with me.'

"That's the seriousness of this, the power of the conversion. I didn't know what was going on. I was listening to the words I was singing, 'You oughta be with me,' realizing that it was like a commitment, a covenant. You oughta be with me. I'm not saying, I wanna seduce you. I'm not talking about our sisters and brothers in a disparaging way. No, no, no."

Green began to hear his own lyrics in a new way, discovering meaning in words he had written years earlier, finding a spiritual significance in love songs that he had never heard before. "I was singing these songs, and just rejoicing to it. 'I'm Still in Love with You,' 'Call Me,' 'Family Reunion Trip,' 'Let's Stay Together.' We're talking about new friends, young friends, old friends, the family. The tree which we were all brought up from.

"At the concerts, when I come offstage, I'm soaking wet. Everything on me is wet. And when I get done ministering, I'm soaking wet. I give as much in both situations, because I'm trying to relate the message to the people. You plant the seed, and the message is always contained in the seed."

When I got up to leave and said, "Thanks very much, Reverend," he laughed a loud, short laugh. "That's okay," he said, "you can call me Al—like Paul Simon says!" And then he danced into his next meeting, clapping his hands and singing as he went.

BILLY BRAGG

The Politics of the Heart

Maybe Billy Bragg was born in the wrong place at the wrong time. Perhaps he would have preferred to have been a compatriot of Woody Guthrie, Pete Seeger, Phil Ochs, or Bob Dylan—folk singers swept to prominence by the tide of history, capturing the issues of the day such as the Depression, the dust bowl, civil rights, or the war in Vietnam. But as it turned out, Bragg came of age in a London suburb called Barking, learning to play guitar as the 1970s dawned, practicing songs by the Rolling Stones in his mother's back room. In 1977 the unknown aspiring songwriter was taught a pivotal lesson by the Clash: it was possible for rock and politics to marry and still have a good time. But it wasn't until the coal miners' strike in 1984, which violently polarized Britain, that Billy Bragg was in the right place at the right time. Thereafter, anti-Thatcher politics became the driving force behind his songwriting, and his iconoclastic act—lone, deeply accented voice accompanied by single electric guitar—became a success.

Although he came to prominence in the heady days of the English new wave, Bragg had little in common with the detached, ironic songcraft of peers like Elvis Costello, Graham Parker, and Nick Lowe. Beyond his stark presentation and his unfashionably earnest singing, what distinguished Bragg was his leftist politics. In 1986 Bragg helped organize a coalition of musicians into the "Red

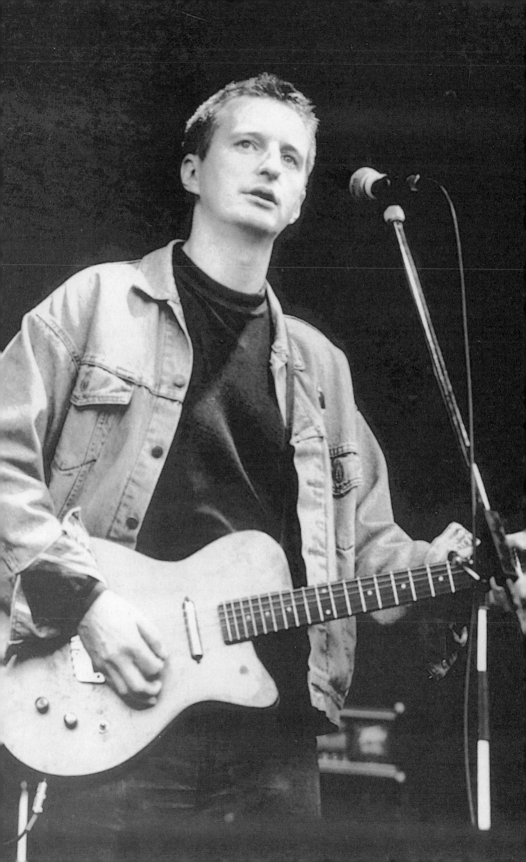

Wedge," which helped to keep young people informed about the Labour Party's positions on various issues. He began to articulate his own ideology as "socialism of the heart," an interpersonal brand of politics in which human relationships are paramount. This may explain why, along with his ardent songs about miners' unions and other political topics, he also composed some achingly delicate love songs. "Levi Stubbs' Tears," for example, tells the tale of a woman in a crumbling relationship, and of the soul singer who looks down from heaven and cries for her. And in "Must I Paint You a Picture," Bragg begs that the mysterious mechanics of love not be dissected like the inner workings of a watch, for fear that, once disassembled, the subtle gears of an intimate relationship may never fit together again. Not exactly the rabble-rousing of your typical socialist union leader.

As the eighties drew to a close and Margaret Thatcher fell from power, Bragg withdrew from recording and performing life for several years, perhaps because he no longer had his archenemy Thatcher to attack. At the same time, his wife gave birth to a son, meaning Bragg the folksinger had to discover ways in which socialism of the heart could apply to Bragg the father and family man.

One of the songs on Bragg's 1996 album, *William Bloke,* is called "Upfield" and narrates William Blake's childhood encounter with angelic beings in a tree on a hill in London. The song typifies the way that, for Bragg, socially conscious themes intersect with spirituality and the romance of everyday life. "In this song I am using the powerful language of gospel music but I am not trying to convey a religious message, although I am using images of angels and so on. But I am trying to convey a spiritual message, which is a very different thing. To me, religion is organized worship, very much regimented rather than something organic. When I want to speak about spirituality, I'm talking about the human spirit that we all have in common. When I use the phrase 'socialism of the heart,' I'm talking about left-wing politics that focus on their humanitarian roots. Even in the most dogmatic, ideological left-wing thought—Marxism, Leninism, Trotskyism—there is still a humanitarian undercurrent, although you don't see it much.

"I came to hold my political beliefs not from reading Marx or any heavy political tomes but because I was looking for an ideological manifestation of my basic humanitarian ideals. Marx thought it would be the industrialized countries who would move toward communism, but unfortunately it was the nonindustrialized countries—both China and the former Soviet Union—who brought industrial revolutions upon themselves in the name of communism, destroying the lives of millions of people. In the face of Marxism's failures, I can return to my humanitarian beliefs, which I find are still as strong and valid as they were when I was articulating them in a purely political way in the 1980s. What socialism means is up for debate. The only way we're going to be able to talk about socialism without having to take on the baggage of Stalin's totalitarianism is by returning to our roots beyond Marx and Lenin and all the other nineteenth- and early twentieth-century thinkers who have defined what socialism means for so many people, both adherents and critics. For Americans who grew up in the cold war period, their points of reference for the way socialism works are either the Soviet Union, China, or maybe the Swedish example. But in Europe we have a much broader and more organic idea of what socialism can be."

Considering his political convictions, one might wonder why Bragg chose to devote himself to a life of singing rather than some more direct form of activism (or better yet, why he isn't slogging it out in the mines alongside his union brethren). "As far as my life's purpose goes, there's a practical side to my career choice: music is the only thing I've ever been any good at, and it took me until I was twenty-five years old to realize that."

Before settling on music, Bragg searched around for other careers, including a stint as a tank driver in the British Royal Armoured Corps. It was a strange career move for a die-hard pacifist such as Bragg, but it provided him with a focus for his postadolescent rebellion, and something that all protest singers need: an up-close and personal encounter with something to protest against. "It was odd, but the army was an opposite side of myself that I needed to explore. I needed something to push against, and my parents weren't around for me to do that. My mother was a widow, so there was no point in pushing against her. I loved her too much. But I needed something, and by entering the volunteer army, I discovered what I really wanted to do, which is the job I do now."

Bragg was writing songs by the time he entered the military, but they were mostly straightforward love tunes. One song recorded for his first album, called "To Have and Have Not," included the lyric "Just because you're better than me doesn't mean I'm lazy," which foreshadowed the sharp class consciousness that would make his best work stand out in the coming years. "I was, at the time, already trying to write songs with a humanitarian, egalitarian philosophy," he says, "but it was very individualistic, very nonideological."

In 1984 Margaret Thatcher reached the peak of her power when she took on England's National Union of Mine Workers. It was a defining political moment in the lives of many people in Bragg's generation in Britain, and it gave him an ideology to match his humanitarian impulse. When Bragg began to perform in the northern English cities most affected by the miners' strike, he was heckled by people who viewed him suspiciously, as a parasitic pop star whose career was thriving on their problems. "These were ordinary left-wing people," Bragg says of his detractors. "They were questioning my motives, and rightly so, too."

It was these left-wing hecklers and critics who forced him to clarify his thoughts, to form a definite political position. "In explaining myself and discussing things with these people, I began to articulate my views in a much more ideological way. I began to define myself as a socialist. Whereas before, in the 1979 election when Thatcher was elected, I didn't even bother to vote. I just wasn't interested. I thought politics were really boring."

Bragg was not raised with politics, protest, or radicalism of any kind in his blood. His father was a self-educated warehouse laborer and his mother, who hardly had any formal education, worked various odd jobs. While Bragg's apolitical upbringing was far from luxurious, neither was he one of the working-class heroes who were the subjects of his songs, the beneficiaries of his fund-raising performances, and in some sense, his personal heroes. "It's hard to define working class in England. I come from a working-class area and a working-class background, and it always seemed to me that working-class people left school at sixteen, and that's what I did. The middle-class people stayed on to get some higher education. But we weren't poor. We were living in an ordinary suburb of London, and I had a very ordinary, nonpolitical upbringing.

"I was a bit of an odd kid at school for listening to Bob Dylan, but the band that changed my life was the Clash. It was the arrival of punk in 1977, and going to see the Clash, and realizing that they were the same age as me and my mates and they were actually doing it! This was incredible, because everyone else making it in music was a generation older than us. The other thing was that the Clash were very, very political. I think the first political thing I ever did, consciously anyway, was to go on a Rock Against Racism march, and that was to see the Clash play at the end of the march. So punk was very political in that sense.

"It was alternative, revolutionary politics I was drawn to. I didn't see any point in getting involved with Labour. But when the miners lost after a year of being on strike, I realized that we don't have a revolutionary process here in Britain, because if there was going to be a revolution, it would have happened during the strike, which was the most powerfully politicizing thing that had happened for generations.

"So at the end of the strike, I thought, okay, what can we do next? I came to the conclusion that maybe the reason the Clash didn't change the world was that they were so naive as to suggest they were going to be able to do it—and I was even more naive to believe them. And perhaps it was their failure to connect with mainstream politics that was the problem."

Bragg's first truly political album was *Talking With the Taxman About Poetry*. His albums were steadily earning gold sales in the United Kingdom and Bragg was developing an increasingly high profile, partly because of his poetics and partly because of his politics. Preparing for the 1987 elections, Bragg decided to organize other like-minded musicians into a political force via the Red Wedge. "We were doing these benefit gigs for everything from Nicaragua, antiracism, Artists Against Apartheid, Miners' Solidarity, and so on, and we were meeting the same bands all the time: Paul Weller, Everything But The Girl, Jimmy Somerville. So we decided to get together and form the Red Wedge, not to tell people to vote for Labour, but to encourage them to find out as much as possible about Labour by stimulating debate in the music press. At the time, Labour had quite a radical platform and for the first time had a leader who had grown up with pop music, Neil Kinnock. He knew that popular music could carry a powerful political message. Whereas Margaret Thatcher had absolutely no understanding of popular culture. This wasn't just about Bill Clinton playing the sax on MTV. It was a real cultural change in this country: for the first time a leader of a political party understood the meaning of the cultural changes that had happened since 1945."

The Red Wedge gave journalists a hook and raised Bragg's profile in the United States even further. The only problem was that magazines were writing about his politics more often than they were focusing on his music. "It's a trade-off," Bragg says. "I want to talk about politics in the paper. I don't want to do my politics in isolation where nobody knows anything about it. So the more people who hear what I have to say, the better. I would much rather be known for my politics than for being like Kiss, because I wore kitty-cat makeup."As Bragg's success continued to grow, another double-edged sword appeared: if he made it to the top as a pop star, would he lose touch with the very people and issues that helped him to succeed? He is slightly evasive on the subject, but it is one that he has given some thought to. "I'm not a believer in living in a garret as a starving artist," he says, "and I have to tell you that I now own more underwear and socks than I've ever had in my life. I don't begrudge anybody who gets to that point financially, but I think the point is, if you get money, then try to think of some good things to do with it. I started up a record label in the eighties and spent a lot of my money trying to help bands make their first records. Money's like horseshit. If you pile it up high, it stinks to high heaven. But if you spread it around a bit, it makes things grow. At the moment, the transition from a bachelor lifestyle to family man has been an expensive venture in itself."

Raising a son has put Bragg's philosophy to the test in several practical ways. His abiding faith in government, for example, may not be so abiding when it comes to putting his son into the state school system. "Say you believe strongly in state education but the state school around here is shit. What are you gonna do? The state school is right next to a huge traffic roundabout, so the air must be full of lead, which will put lead in his brain. The point is, all these years you've only had to worry about yourself. Parenthood brings in a lot of gray areas, and it means you can't live in a black-and-white world anymore.

"Life is full of ambiguities, and life does offer compromises all the time. The important thing to try to do is ensure that the compromises we have to make are made on our terms. There are a lot of people who do this job in order to escape reality, people who want to be closed off to the world. They buy a big mansion or do a lot of drugs or all those other things to opt out, instead of getting engaged. Where is your point of engagement with the society you're in? Is it just with your maid?"

In the chorus of one of Bragg's songs, called "Life with the Lions," he sings, "I hate the asshole I've become every time I see you." It is this self-deprecation and self-doubt that make him so difficult to criticize—he has already done that for you in his songs. "As someone who's had my share of arguments, one of my favorite human characteristics is doubt. I'd rather talk to someone who can question themselves rather than people who are sure they've got all the bloody answers.

"As a songwriter, whether it's a political song or a love song, you are trying to create a common bond with the listener. Now, if you point out something you've done wrong, you're striking a chord with the listener and making them feel that perhaps they're not the only person in the world in a quandary. Because although we all have totally different experiences on a day-to-day basis, the way these experiences make us feel joyful or embarrassed or awkward is very similar. If you can reach inside yourself and find a metaphor to conjure up these deep human feelings, you will strike a common chord with a lot of listeners. Of course, you don't do this consciously. Every now and then, you write something that metaphorically says something about a lot of things all at once and that gets right in past people's defenses. It's something that one cannot do intentionally, but it's a source of great satisfaction when you do it. The human condition is the most fascinating and complex thing to try and get at in a song."

LEONARD COHEN
The Unbearable Panic of Being

In the realm of pop music, which is usually about entertaining people with a catchy melody and a beat they can dance to, Leonard Cohen is an unlikely candidate. Cohen, a widely respected poet and novelist whose career as a recording artist started with the 1967 album *The Songs of Leonard Cohen*, has consistently plumbed the depths of melancholy with a seriousness verging on the Talmudic.

His voice, a warm, deep bass that sounds like a boot stepping on wet gravel, isn't the typical tone you hear blasting out of radios. It's more like something you hear coming from deep in the belly of a chanting monk—which is appropriate, since Cohen is now a monk at a Zen center in the mountains near Los Angeles. While he has never been a household name in America, his music has earned a considerable following throughout Europe (there is, for example, an annual Leonard Cohen festival in Poland), and each of his albums sells more than a million copies worldwide. The upside of his relative lack of success in America is that it has enabled him to experiment artistically without much pressure from his U.S.-based record company. There is a (perhaps apocryphal) tale of an encounter he had with Walter Yetnikoff, then head of CBS Records, in which Yetnikoff is said to have remarked, "I know you're great, Cohen, but I just don't know if you're any good."

Leonard Cohen was raised in Montreal in a relatively well-to-do Jewish household, and although he has been a student of Buddhism since the early 1970s, like Allen Ginsberg did, he views Buddhism as a way of illuminating his Judaism rather than as an alternative to it. Visitors to Cohen's room at the Mount Baldy Zen Center have been confused by symbols of his Jewish faith, which are still very much in evidence. "Some people are very surprised to find a menorah and the Sabbath candles in my room. But there's no conflict for me between my family religion and my studying or acquiring these insights through another discipline. My teacher often emphasizes that Zen is not a religion. It's a practice, the end of which is to manifest itself as true Love.

"I grew up in an observant family and the synagogue was part of my life. I bought my first guitar at a secondhand store and I played piano and clarinet in the high school. My friends were learning instruments, and whenever we had a moment, we played music together. My mother had a beautiful contralto voice and she sang Russian and Jewish folk songs around the house, so I've always been deeply involved in music."

As a child, Cohen didn't have any overtly mystical or spiritual experience of Judaism, but the music of the synagogue always affected him deeply. "A chill would often go down my spine when the cantor began singing and at other emotional moments in the service. So, during my childhood, much of my idea of music was connected with the idea of a liturgy and of a supplication. I didn't identify it as such, but the connection of music and high seriousness was always there. So music has been central to my life, and I've always felt that the success of my own written work is musical. I always hear an invisible guitar behind my novels and poetry. In other words, I never got very far from those influences."

In 1954, when Cohen was twenty years old, he formed his first band, the Buckskin Boys, for which he played guitar. "I was writing little things here and there, but we weren't performing any of my songs yet, we were performing square-dance music. So I've always had some kind of life as a musician. In fact, I came to poetry through the lyric rather than the other way around; it was my interest in folk music that led me into poetry. It's sort of like, the good music on the right is country music and the good music on the left is rap music, and both of them have a high investment in the seriousness of the lyric and both examine deep emotions and concerns. It was easy for me to get into rap in the same way it was easy for me to get into country."

It was Cohen's second book, 1961's *The Spice Box of Earth*, that first brought him recognition and won him a Canada Council grant. With the grant money he traveled to Europe to visit the ancient capitals, Rome, Athens, and Jerusalem, and eventually the Greek island of Hydra, where he bought a house and settled down to write for several years.

While Cohen worked on his prose in Greece, the American music scene was changing. Dylan was breaking through to mass audiences, proving that literate folk rock could be economically viable. "When I came back from Greece in the mid-sixties and heard the so-called folk song renaissance going on with Joan Baez and Dylan, I thought there was an opportunity to make a living. I'd already published a couple of novels, and I couldn't meet my bills. This folk thing had already hit the marketplace in some way and it didn't seem too different from the music I was doing, so maybe I could find some way to make a living. It was mostly economic urgency that propelled me into the marketplace. I was already doing the music; I was playing harmonica before I heard Dylan."

When Cohen returned to North America in 1964, he began going down to New York, often borrowing the money to make the trip from Montreal. He had heard about the scene in Greenwich Village, but after hanging out in cafés there with people dressed in berets and black sweaters he became disgusted with the armies of superficial hepcats. One day, while sitting by himself in a coffeeshop, be picked up a napkin and wrote "Kill cool" on it. It was the end of his illusions about New York's hip arty crowd.

"Around then I was introduced to Judy Collins; she liked some of the work I was doing but wanted to hear more. Then I finished the song 'Suzanne,' and I sang it to her over the telephone and she liked it very much." Collins recorded "Suzanne," and on the basis of its minor success, Cohen was able to secure an interview with John Hammond Sr., head of A&R at Columbia Records. "I played a few songs for him and he said, 'You got it!' I didn't know whether he meant that I was allowed to number myself among the great ones that he'd discovered, or whether he just meant I had a recording contract." Cohen did get a contract with Columbia and began what he calls his "curious career" as a singer.

By the time *The Songs of Leonard Cohen* was released in 1967, many of the rock intelligentsia were gaining their first exposure to Eastern religions. Cohen wasn't yet interested in Buddhist teachings, and in some way he still isn't: "I still don't have much interest in Buddhism, in any formal way. I bumped into a man in California who impressed me. His name was Joshu Sasaki Roshi, and he happened to be a Rinzai monk. I often say that if the man

I met had been, say, a professor of physics in Heidelberg, I would've learned German and studied physics."

After the release of Cohen's first album, he began a period of relentless touring. Two studio albums followed: *Songs From A Room* (1969) and *Songs of Love and Hate* (1971). As his recording career picked up pace, so did his drinking and depression, and in the early 1970s, Cohen began studying with Joshu Sasaki, doing *sesshins,* the rigorous meditation practice retreats of the Rinzai Zen Buddhist sect. "It was extremely formal—or at least super- ficially formal on the outside, and very warm and wild on the inside. You don't get into a practice that severe unless you're in some kind of trouble. I was in plenty of trouble. I had a great sense of dis-ease and distress. I was living all over the place, which was part of the trouble. So I found that this institution, called the *sesshin,* was well de- signed for me.

"The *sesshin* lasts seven days. It takes place about once a month, and you sit, with breaks, from three in the morning to about nine-thirty at night. This particular kind of training could be likened to educating a swimmer by throwing him into the pool. You wouldn't do this unless there was a deep love between you and your teacher and a great sense of comradeship among you and your fellow practitioners. So, as I say, you're not going to do this prac- tice unless you're in trouble and unless you experience love."

Sitting for fifteen hours a day without much grounding in Buddhist philosophy or study allowed Cohen to encounter his mind in a very direct way. When you are engaged in this kind of meditation, the experience of your own mind can be frightening, enraging, and ex- hausting. There is no distraction and there is no quitting. There is nowhere to turn but inward, so you sit and observe whatever comes up: self-deceptions, anger, lust, hopes, fears, fantasies, even hallucinations. It requires immense patience and perseverance, and after a series of stops and starts with his meditation practice, Cohen eventually began to feel some lessening of his interior panic. "I would have various experiences, but the cumulative effect was a certain sense that you can work this thing out, just a certain sense that there is a way out."

This sense of spaciousness and workability represented a much-needed alleviation of a lifelong existential crisis. In a 1995 conversation with Anjelica Huston published in *Interview* magazine, Cohen described the mindset with which he approached Buddhist practice: "It was mostly panic from one moment to the next. And nothing much else was going on. And any of the decisions that I made, if one could actually locate a shape or form, were all within a wall, the landscape of panic.

"Meditation is very, very physical. In the old practice there was no word for experience. The phrase was 'attaining in the body.' The point was that no idea is going to come and transform you. The transformation was going to be experienced . . . cellularly. This particular school of Zen has always considered itself the Marines of the spiritual world, so it has a kind of bias against conceptual thinking in favor of a very rigorous physical life.

"Nothing can stop you from thinking. The human mind is designed to think continually. Something I wrote quite a few years ago was, 'The voices in my head, they don't care what I do, they just want to argue the matter through and through.' It is a common mistake, to think you're going into some kind of spiritual practice and you're going to be relieved of the human burdens, from human crosses like thought, jealousy, despair—in fact, if anything, these feelings are amplified.

"There is a place for ideas and scholarship in the Rinzai tradition and there's certainly no real bias against it. The practice is rigorous in that it demands that you experience yourself."

The experience of sitting face-to-face with your neuroses, anxiety, anger, fear, and all the other aspects of mind that you'd prefer not to acknowledge is at the heart of Buddhist practice. It also became an integral part of Cohen's maturation as a songwriter and performer. Spurred on by a comment his roshi made, Cohen delved even more deeply into the dark emotions that his early work hinted at, and he eventually discovered some redemption there. "When I was recording the album *New Skin for the Old Ceremony*—it must have been 1972—my roshi came to the recording session in New York, and the next morning I asked him what he thought of it. At this time I was being widely regarded as a kind of depressive. The joke was that they sold razor blades with my records because they felt that I was so melancholic and an insufferable self-pitier. Those observations were occurring in review after review. So I asked Roshi what he thought of the recording session and he said, 'You should sing more sad.'

"I thought, it's right, it's true, it's true, I'm just skirting the edges of my true feelings. It was an encouragement to dive in. To follow the emotions to where they really lead. I think of it in a physical sense, in that I have to plunge in. To plunge into my life, into my work, because the reticence, shyness, and bashfulness, all these hampering strategies really prevent the song from unfolding."

Cohen's relationship with his roshi at one point seemed to resemble that of two drinking buddies as much as it did the traditional teacher/student relationship. But while Cohen has never sworn off alcohol completely, his roshi has been a tempering influence.

"I remember sitting with him in the dressing room before a concert in Hamburg, in the seventies, and I was drinking a full tumbler of cognac before the performance. I remember him hitting my thigh with his hand, hard, and saying to me, 'Body important!'

"I've eased off it, because he's eased off it. We used to drink a lot with meals, but he's become much more attentive to his physical person now, because he's determined to stick around for a while, so we're not drinking as much now. Sake was one of his preferred drinks, but he had his gallbladder removed recently, and somehow the alcohol goes swiftly into the bloodstream without the gallbladder, so he gets the effect with just a few sips now."

While monastic life may in theory leave room for some of life's visceral pleasures, the realities of the rigorous schedule make sleep the most sought-after indulgence. "There's very little time for anything when you're actually following the schedule of the Zen center, but you can do what you want to do. In the Zen wedding ceremony, there's a moment when the couple is presented with a number of precepts they have to affirm, and one of them is the precept against intoxication. Then it goes on to say that not being ignorant is considered as observing the precept against intoxication, and immediately the sake is served to the couple and the guests."

With regard to the ways that life in the monastery may have transformed him as a person and an artist, Cohen is circumspect. "It's hard to say. When one changes, one grows, one retreats. You're in a continual flux of strategies and activities, so while it's a nice idea to try to organize your life or have a goal of liberation or enlightenment, in the actual daily activity, these strategies are not really useful."

Enlightenment, according to Cohen, is nothing

other than true love. And like enlightenment, he views love as eternal. As he told Anjelica Huston, "I think love lasts. I think it's the nature of love to last. I think it's eternal, but I think we don't know what to do with it much of the time. Because of its eternal and mysterious qualities, our panicked responses to it are inappropriate and often tragic. But the thing itself, when it can be appropriately assimilated into the landscape of panic, is the only redeeming possibility for human beings."

It is because love has such a singular redemptive power, Cohen argues, that falling in love—falling out of loneliness—is so traumatic. "Because we are awakening from the dream of isolation, from the dream of loneliness, it's a terrible shock. It's a delicious, terrible shock that none of us knows what to do with. You dissolve your sentries and your battalions for a moment and you really do see that there is this unfixed, free-flowing energy of emotion and thought between people, that it really is there. It's tangible, and you can almost ride on it into another person's breast. Your heart opens, and of course you're completely panicked because you're used to guarding this organ with your life."

In light of this, Cohen believes that one of the highest callings of the musician (or artists in general, what he calls cultural workers) is to prepare people for love. "I think that is the ocean in which we're all swimming. We all want to dissolve. We all need that experience of forgetting who we are. I think that's what love is—you forget who you are. Forgetting who you are is such a delicious experience and so frightening. So we're in this conflicted predicament: we want it but we really can't support it. So I think that what our education and culture should be for is preparing the heart for that journey outside the cage of the ribs."

Cohen moved to Mount Baldy as a full-time resident about three years ago and describes his recent ordination as "a kind of formality, since I'd been around for so long." Although rumors circulated that it was his breakup with actress Rebecca DeMornay, Cohen maintains that his motive for entering the monastic life full-time had more to do with an appreciation of his teacher's mortality. "At a certain point a few years ago, I became very much aware of my teacher's age. I decided to take advantage of the time that he had available. That was the major motive for living here full-time."

These days he rises at 2:30 in the morning and spends his time taking care of his roshi. "I'm cooking for the old man, so I have three meals a day to prepare for him, and whatever he gets, the monks eat with us. So I really have a life as a cook right now. And we do about six hours a day of meditation, plus a day of work. We don't really discuss the dharma too much, but there is a *sesshin* once a month.

"Right now my post is the secretary to the roshi, that's what it's called in this tradition. I'm also the chauffeur. There are three of us who do this job on rotation, just looking after the old guy. He's ninety now, and we're just keeping him around as long as we can. He's in the most passionate and articulate phase that I've ever seen him in. Physically, he's pretty good. He threatens to live until 120, until he can bring some of us to maturity."

Between the long hours of meditation and the daily chores and service to his roshi, Cohen still finds time to write and record. He has a primitive computer and a synthesizer in his two-room cabin on Mount Baldy, where he can work out musical ideas and do basic demos. From practicing meditation that reveals the illusory nature of self, he makes the transition to composing songs that re-

veal an agonizing obsession with self. "You can't ever dissolve the 'I'—for any long period of time, anyway. As Roshi
says, 'You can't live in God's world for very long; there's
no restaurants and no toilets.' So while there is a notion
that there is an ego to be dissolved, that's questionable. In
any case, you need an ego to participate and interact with
all the other egos in the human life. So it's not a matter of
dissolving, smashing, or annihilating the ego. You need an
ego. You just need to be able to move gracefully from one
position to another, from the position of life to death. If
you find yourself in a prison, you know, there's a way to
live graciously in a prison, but there's no point in denying
that it's a prison. We are often in a prison, and it's important to recognize it and treat it like a home.

"We live in a human world; there is a human culture that we are all part of, and if you're interested in par-
ticipating in any way, modest or not, then you've got to
express yourself in terms that the culture understands. So,
you know, on the surface, a song like 'Your Cheating
Heart,' may seem deficient in some kind of profundity, but
it isn't really—it really is a song of the heart."

THE REVEREND RUN

Born Again and Still Illin'

Certain parts of certain American ghettos have an almost rural feel. Paterson, New Jersey, has a neighborhood like that. There are still plenty of wooden houses, slowly sagging, with the paint curling off the boards, buildings that seem perched on the cusp between the rural South and the urban North. New York City is just a few miles up the highway but far away in terms of culture, economy, and sense of time. On one Sunday morning recently, there was more than the usual number of cars parked on the torn-up grass next to the New Christian Missionary Church. The church is a white industrial-looking structure located in a strip of crumbling wooden buildings, across the street from a small copse. The guest preacher that day was a man who led a revolution in music. The Reverend Run (Joseph Simmons) was one of rap's founding fathers as a member of Run-DMC, but he turned to the church after his career and private life ran into trouble.

Run had come out from his expansive home in Jamaica Estates, Queens, in a shiny black late-model Mercedes, and had been sitting in front of the church for an hour before it opened. He was hired by the church in an attempt to bring younger people back into the fold. Perhaps Run's presence explained why, unlike old-school churches where "Sunday best" is still the tradition, a lot of the people in the pews were dressed in baggy street clothes.

Three heavyset dark-skinned women with starched white gloves led parishioners to their seats. The three-hour-long service began with a few tunes by the choir and an interpretive dance by eight little girls wearing matching African-print skirts, their performance made poignant by the distinctly unpolished musical accompaniment—a cassette player held up to the deacon's microphone. When Reverend Run approached the podium, dressed in an expensive black suit and shiny shoes, his head shaved to a clean, glimmering pate, he looked slightly nervous, as though he were still unsure of what tone his sermon should take.

Unfortunately, Run's microphone technique hadn't changed since the days when he was rocking the crowd at Latin Quarters, and when he started to preach, he overwhelmed the church's meager public address system by pressing the mike to his mouth like a crazed emcee and dropping biblical science in a blur of distortion, rending his sermon slightly unintelligible.

Run is a man of intense energy and single-pointed concentration, and he paced the stage like a panther, taking a few steps to one side and then turning sharply back in the other direction, speaking with hypnotic, rhythmic phrasing. He started out on safe ground, affirming that Jesus had indeed changed his life and that he owed all praise to God. Then he asked the congregation (which he occasionally referred to as the audience) to open their Bibles to Luke and read a passage wherein Jesus is asked whether it's kosher to heal on the Sabbath, when all work is forbidden. Jesus, using a typically Jewish debate technique, answers by asking a question: "If your ass or oxen fell in a hole, would you wait until after the Sabbath to save the animal?" At the end of the passage Run paused and shut the Bible. Then he began shouting into the mike: "WHAT

I AM SAYING TO YOU IS, IF YOUR ASS IS IN A HOLE, YOU GOT A RIGHT TO GET YOUR ASS OUT THE HOLE!" Many of the older church people were visibly shocked, and Run backed off, explaining that he wasn't using profanity. "An ass is an animal," he said, "but it could be your career, or your life that's in a hole."

Run got personal then. He recounted the story of his own conversion, describing how, as his album sales peaked at four million, and then dropped to two million, and then plummeted to two hundred thousand, he began to feel that something was wrong with his life. As evidence that he had once again become a success since he found God, he cited the $300,000 budget of an upcoming music video he was going to shoot with the rap group Bones, Thugs, and Harmony.

Later, when I asked about the irony of using material success as the measuring stick of spiritual attainment, Run pointed out that the reason so many young people have rejected the message of the church is that they associate their parents' and grandparents' adherence to church life with poverty. Because of that, Run reasoned, the poorer segments of our society cannot yet afford the luxury of a purely spiritual message, and during the sermon he had taken great pains to prove that Jesus did not ask anybody to be poor, asserting that Jesus was a wealthy man. As evidence he pointed to the fact that at his crucifixion people stood in line for a strip of Christ's garment, which Run suggested was the "Versace" of the era.

"You know why I emphasized the material side?" he asked me later. "Because black people in the Baptist church are riding around broke and they can't pay their rent. I'm trying to teach them that Jesus wasn't teaching people to be broke, and being spiritually blessed doesn't mean having to cry every night about the electricity and the water being shut off. I was trying to share with them the principles of tithing and the way that it can help you in the material realm. Money is very important while you're here in this earthly realm because we're not walking around as spirits: we have to eat and we have to pay our bills. Spirituality is good, but we're made of flesh, too. You can walk around with your head in the clouds and be as spiritual as you want, but if you don't have enough money to afford a life, then you might as well have never been made into flesh.

"If there's one thing I'll do as a preacher, I'll try to teach my black people who have been oppressed over the years the principles that Jesus left behind. To show them that Abraham and Joseph and all the Bible greats—none of them were broke. God wants you to be prosperous. So my emphasis will always be on getting your life together in the material realm."

Run feels that if he doesn't emphasize his own financial success, he will be deemed irrelevant by the very audience he is trying to reach. To be a spiritual role model in hip-hop, he argues, you have to portray wealth as an admirable and attainable goal.

"I don't want them to focus on the pie in the sky. I can never get black youth to listen if I say, 'I'm Run, I came to Jesus, and now I'm broke. Come with me to Jesus and be broke, too.' My message is, 'I came to God and my God is a good God.' It would be hard to get people to look up to me if I tell them I'm not doing well. I don't understand those pentecostal people living in the projects with roaches in their rooms, trying to preach to their kids, 'You better stop what you're doing and come to Jesus,' and they're broke. The old lady trying to preach to her son about how good Jesus is, and all he ever sees is her being broke.

"Christianity has for so long been perverted into the

idea that to be with Jesus you gotta take a vow of poverty, and that's not the truth. Jesus was not broke. They were truly casting lots for what he had on. At least it should be a matter of choice. A lot of people have made money, and if they wanna take a vow of poverty, that's fine, but my people cannot afford to make that decision yet. Let them get rich and *then* say they don't wanna be rich, let them make that decision. They may find that being rich doesn't make them happy, but they're *definitely* not gonna be happy if they don't even have money for the basics. I'm talking about my people, living right now in the Bronx projects, and they're saying, 'Mommy's praising Jesus all week but then at the end of the week we can't eat. So I'm gonna go sell crack.' So all I'm trying to do is teach my people the true principles that Christ taught."

But Run's sermon was not only about the importance of having fat pockets. He also waxed slightly mystical, with a tale that expressed both his wonderment and his humility at having put his life into God's hands. The night that Tupac Shakur was fatally shot in Las Vegas, Run was in a hotel room nearby, desperately trying to get in touch with the rapper and his confidant, Suge Knight. Run had flown out to Vegas to see the Tyson fight, but because of minor last-minute confusion, he missed the fight and was unable to get in touch with Shakur. He recounted this anecdote as evidence of the way God has protected him, and of the need to surrender one's will to a higher power. The sermon ended with a seamless shift into decidedly spiritual terms: you cannot receive without giving, he said, after reading a passage from Malachi on tithing. "You cannot get love without giving it."

It was the assassination of Martin Luther King Jr. by a white supremacist in 1968 that undermined the role of the black church for generations of young black men to come. The church's teaching that by "turning the other cheek" and practicing nonviolent resistance, blacks could attain justice in American society was viewed by militant factions as naive. Hence the appeal of Louis Farrakan and other preachers of the Nation of Islam who use racist incitements to violence to lure dispossessed young men into their ranks. Run lays some of the responsibility for this trend on the black churches, which for too many years failed to engage their members in active self-help programs.

"Militant people are not hearing what the church is trying to say because of the church's history of passivity and message of weakness and saying people should live in poverty and let others beat you up. I wouldn't expect a Muslim to respect a church like that, and that's not what God wants you to be like. The church's messages, such as 'Turn the other cheek,' can't be read by the letter, they have to be read by the spirit. It wasn't just 'Turn the other cheek, get beat up, and be broke.' That's not what Jesus meant at all, and that's all I'm saying. My message will always be a message of health and prosperity. That's what God wants: he don't want you to be broke and he don't want you to be sick. He wants you to be able to provide for your family.

"You shouldn't wait for your pie in the sky. You can have it now. With ice cream, too. The church always said, 'We don't worry about material things now. Jesus has got the mansion for us in the sky.' But why'd God even put you here if that's the case? The point is, God wants you to prosper and be in good health."

As a front man for Run-DMC, Run certainly followed the admonition about prospering: Run-DMC was the first rap act to appear on MTV, the first to have a number-one single on the *Billboard* charts, the first to have a gold album, the first to have a platinum album, and the first to win a contract for product endorsement. Their 1986 *Raising Hell* album featured a duet with Aerosmith on "Walk This Way" that presaged a trend of rap and rock fusion.

Although Run-DMC was far from the first rap group, they were the first to show black kids (and soon white ones, too) that rappers could be superstars. With their black leather outfits and their thick gold rope chains, they proved that rappers could be style trendsetters in the same way rock stars were. They scored an endorsement contract from Adidas on their own, distinctly black, terms at a time when Michael Jackson was rapidly sacrificing his blackness on his rise to pop stardom. Because they were simultaneously mass market and street credible, Run-DMC provided the inspiration for an entire generation of emcees to enter the rap game, and there are few rappers active today who do not acknowledge a debt of inspiration to them.

When Run-DMC's *King of Rock* hit the airwaves back in 1985, it delivered a creative jolt to the development of one of the most innovative musical forms since bebop. A lot of rap songs may sound derivative and familiar today, but in the early and mid-1980s, Run-DMC was creating truly new music, mixing blustery, balls-to-the-wall arena rock guitar with monolithic drumbeats and call-and-response tag-team rhyming.

At the time that Run-DMC emerged, rap production was relatively simple; tracks were far less dense than they became under the creative leadership of producers like Hank Shocklee (Public Enemy, Ice Cube), DJ Muggs (House of Pain, Cypress Hill), and the Dust Brothers (Beastie Boys, Beck). By the time "Run's House" was released in 1988, Run-DMC was leading the trend toward more layered recordings, and the track still sounds contemporary, with its slicing turntables and the staccato vocal cadences Run and his partner in rhyme, DMC, perfected. Even then, long before his immersion in Christianity, Run was rapping against guns and violence: "My name is Run, my son / number one for fun / not a gun, that's dumb . . ." he chanted in "Run's House."

While many of the rap pioneers who originally inspired Run, such as Kurtis Blow and Grand Master Flash, came from harsh, poverty-stricken neighborhoods in the Bronx, Run was raised in a stable middle-class neighborhood in Queens. His father was a college professor who taught black history, and his mother worked with children through the New York City parks system. But by the time his career as a rapper took off, he wasn't exactly a regular churchgoing type. "Getting high was very important to me then. Smoking reefer was the most important thing in the world. I'd wake up and get a dollar in my pocket, and if DMC had a dollar, and another person in Hollis had a dollar, we would buy a bag of reefer. My life was all about gettin' high and turntables. I wasn't praying because I felt that God was on my side. I felt that I wasn't doing anything wrong."

Even back in the days when Run was a fifteen-year-old pothead on the streets of Hollis, he had a basic belief in the golden rule and never gave in to the bitches-ho's-Glocks-and-Tecs ethos of gangsta rap. "It was about gettin' high, but it was definitely about being good, too. I always felt that God was not gonna bless me if I was not good to people. Basically, I tried to be as good as I could."

In the late 1970s, Run's older brother, Russell, had begun managing a rapper called Kurtis Blow, and Run had gotten his break as an opening act under the name Son of Kurtis Blow. Soon he joined forces with Jam Master

Jay (Jason Mizell), a deejay, and MC Darryl "D" McDan-
iels. After being rejected by all major labels, the group
signed a contact with the pioneering but controversial rap
label Profile records, for twenty-five hundred dollars. In
June 1983, they released their first album, which stayed on
the charts for a year and became the first gold rap album.
The next year they followed with *King of Rock* but it was
1986's *Rasing Hell* that cemented their status as crossover
stars, with sales bolstered by a blistering performance on
Saturday Night Live. "As we kept getting bigger, I believed
that because I was doing good for people, God was blessing
me. I was watching my day, making sure I didn't hurt nobody, being very conscious of being good to people. Helping an old lady across the street. That type of thing. I just
was in a vibe of doing good."

But when Run-DMC's album sales began to drop
off, Run started to feel less sure about the fact that he was
"blessed," or even on the right path. One day in 1991, Run
walked into a church at the Doral Inn at the suggestion of
one of his bodyguards. "Things were getting so messed up
around me and I felt so bad that I decided to go to church.
I was feeling needful, needing help and direction. I went
for help. I went to find out some things. I was ready.
Things were caving in on me. I just said, it's over. I'm
going to church. I just said, God, I need you.

"The day I walked into that church I was born
again. For a couple of months after I was still smokin'; I
had to fight it off. I knew some of the things in my life
wasn't right, like smoking and profanity, so I had to slowly
get rid of them. It wasn't about becoming a reverend, it
was about just being a member. I became an usher at the
Zoe Ministry Church, seating people. Then I became a
deacon. It was all about servanthood and being dedicated.
I kept going to church, and the bishop watched my walk,

seen what I was learning, and so I began to preach as a deacon on some Sundays. And through that dedication I became a minister."

Run got more and more deeply into the church, but things got worse before they got better. His first wife, Valerie Simmons, left him, taking their three children with her. "She wasn't part of the church, she didn't care about my conversion to Christ. Maybe it was coming anyway, maybe she was ready to leave anyway. It was obvious that things were coming down around me. It was like a Job situation: I was doing all the right things but things were still going wrong. I was still ushering and fasting a lot. My life was caving in on me, so I just kept on going to church every time the door was open. The church became my love. I was fasting and praying, not eating for forty days and forty nights, getting deep into God, just letting it get all down, deep in my soul."

Subsisting mainly on juice and water, Run dropped from 215 pounds to 160. He endured skepticism from his friends and his fans alike. "Everybody thought it was a joke at first, like I was bugging out. But I kept performing and doing my thing. I was waiting for things to turn around and I knew they were gonna. I was gettin' with my God. It was a beautiful thing. I was praying and fasting and speaking in tongues and having angels all around me. It was deep.

"Speaking in tongues is something you have control of. It ain't like the spirit gotta come over you and start moving your mouth like a puppet. You're praying about things that nobody understands but God. It's your own private prayer language. In the Bible it talks about people speaking in unknown tongues. It's your own secret code. You're praying for things that you don't even know you need to be praying for.

"One man said that insanity is doing the same thing over and over and expecting new results. How did my life get better? It was through finding the Lord thy God and his principles. I found the true and living God who led me to principles and to keys, to wisdom and faith and love. Do unto others as you would want done to you. I do a lot of tithing and giving, because life is all give and take. My number-one business in life is giving. If you want a breath, you have to give a breath to get one. Same thing with money, same thing with love, same thing with everything. Anything you want, give a piece of it and you'll get it. You want people to respect you, you need to give respect. You want to become a big-time entertainer, you need to help somebody else become one. You want honor? Honor others. You want a compliment? Go give out compliments. Life is give and take. It's a law, and it works. All truths are parallel.

"A lot of people won't agree with anything I say. A lot of people think spirituality and material things have nothing in common. But I'd like to teach people how to take care of themselves. And not the basics: you can have more, you can have whatever it is that you want. But definitely not at the expense of others. You shouldn't get so caught up in the money thing that you lose sight of Jesus, and loving and caring and all the other principles. That can happen. But I'm definitely on a mission to pull my people up, and I'll be happy to be condemned for it. It really doesn't matter, that's what I'm here to preach.

"In all situations, you reap what you sow. I just sowed a breath so I can reap a breath. In and out. Karma. Life is seedtime and harvest. Sow a seed, reap a harvest. Smack somebody in the back of the head, somebody's gonna hit you in the head with a bat. Sometimes it comes back a little harder, too. Cause and effect. That's all. That's how I feel."

ROBYN HITCHCOCK

Sex, Death, Irony, and Insects

Robyn Hitchcock, unlike most stars, did not get rich when he finally made it big. He grew up that way. Not filthy rich, but certainly well-to-do, in a London household where the garden parties were peopled by academics and intellectuals, and where the young Hitchcock could develop an overactive vocabulary and a fascination with insects, both of which can be heard in his songs today. As leader of the eighties smart-rock quartet the Soft Boys, Hitchcock set quirky subject matter—a man with a woman's shadow, various arachnid-related narratives—to likable pop melodies. After leaving the Soft Boys in 1981, Hitchcock emerged as a solo artist, working both with and without his backing band, the Egyptians.

In 1989 Hitchcock had a hit on American college radio charts with "Queen Elvis." The song, now an annoyingly catchy new wave antique, doesn't represent his best work, which has the capacity to draw listeners in with lyrics that function like weird slice-of-life snapshots. His songs ask funny philosophical questions, offering the pop tune as existential short story.

With the release of *Moss Elixir* and a new 9-CD retrospective of his work, and an upcoming documentary about him directed by Jonathan Demme (the director is a longtime fan), Hitchcock's place as a serious artist is assured, even if he never tops the charts again.

Death is a recurring theme in Hitchcock's work. His songs are not religious, but they are spiritual, in the sense that he uses them to ask personal questions about the universe and our place in it. "Death is the last present that everybody unwraps," Hitchcock says. "It's the one that they leave till midnight on Christmas day, but you have to unwrap it sometime. You can't leave the room without unwrapping it. It's the gift that everybody has to open but nobody asks for."

Hitchcock's songs have plenty of hooks and catchy choruses, but even his love songs seem to wear a philosopher's quizzical grin. Outside a Woody Allen movie, a Robyn Hitchcock album is the most likely place to hear questions of love and death raised side by side. "If there was no death then there would be no sex. We only need sex because we have to replace ourselves. Reproduction was the function of sex initially, as we know, but maybe it's changed now. Maybe sex is a form of communication, a form of expression, a form of abuse, even a form of comedy. It's developed in lots of ways, but originally sex was there so that living things could replace themselves. Sex was the means by which death was cheated.

Hitchcock's music returns repeatedly to the vortex where sex and death come together. He considers those two subjects—rather than love—the most fertile areas for artists to explore. "I'd have thought all songwriters would be writing about sex and death—those are the two main concerns. Romantic love can be enduring or it can be fleeting. Love isn't a gift, whereas sex and death are gifts. Whether we love each other is a moot point. What is certain is that at the end of every day we are one step closer to our own oblivion. We're all going to be kicked through that door, and no one has ever come back through it. Maybe Jesus did, but maybe he was something different when he came back, maybe it wasn't Jesus anymore. Who knows? Either way, that's not enough to make me get down and worship Jesus."

Hitchcock became aware of his own mortality very early on, growing up in a household where he was exposed not only to the life-and-death realities of the natural sciences but also to the manmade ravages of history. "I used to see all these pictures of wars in books my parents had lying around, these cartoons depicting skulls everywhere, and Hieronymus Bosch and stuff like that. I grew up in the shadow of the skull. But I think the other thing that you have to emphasize is that of all the musicians you have talked to, I have had the easiest life. I've probably had only one person who was close to me die in forty-three years, I've never been punched out, I've never been badly ill, I've never been financially destitute. I've had a very comfortable existence."

One thing Hitchcock's privileged upbringing did not afford him was the sense of being completely at ease with himself, nor was it a palliative for existential anxiety. "I feel like the person by the campfire who's being stalked by the eyes winking out in the darkness. You know something's out there but it hasn't got you yet. Every so often you hear something screaming in the bushes—even where I live you hear howling at night and you know that something's being killed by something else, but you don't know what it is. I think I'm probably the perfect example of the pampered bourgeois who knows all this stuff is out there but it hasn't happened to him yet."

For all his philosophizing, Hitchcock doesn't know how his life as an imaginative, introspective person has affected him as a musician. "Stuff just filters through, doesn't it? You live and it comes out in your work. It's in your handwriting. But what really matters is your state of mind when you die. You might have lived quite an evil life but never realized it; you might die a contented person because nothing has ever challenged your way of behaving. Or you might have been a good person, but you still are dissatisfied with yourself. So I'm interested whether there is some point where you pass through the vale and they show you what you really were like. I've always thought that when you die perhaps your consciousness is played back to you and you have to judge it."

On the liner notes to *Moss Elixir*, Hitchcock wrote a short story about going through the experience of dying and discovering a leap in physical evolution—the opening of the third eye—which brings about a corresponding leap in consciousness. The result is the kind of panoramic sensitivity and unconditional compassion that is the goal of many world religions. But Hitchcock prefers to speculate about such sci-fi spiritual scenarios rather than sit down and attempt to bring them about in his own life. One reason Hitchcock remains just a dreamer, deeply interested in but forever on the sidelines of spiritual practice, is that he believes that humanity is not yet capable of transformation and enlightenment.

"My theory is that humanity is doomed unless we make some kind of evolutionary leap. I can't see us going around and around in the same agonies indefinitely. As technology improves, sooner or later the whole thing will rub itself out, or we will rub it out, in which case we'll probably take everything else with us. I believe that the earth is a form of intelligence. It's Gaia, which is life, or God, if you know what I mean. It isn't a moral sort of thing; it's just that generally life works itself out. Gaia is the idea that the whole world is a living intelligent organism. Nature generally manages to regulate itself, but every so often something crops up like the human that doesn't really fit in. I think something will physically evolve in us. In my story, I suggest that it's a third eye opening—that the skin on your forehead rips open and a new eyeball pokes through, and with that new eyeball you can really see and empathize with other people. It's kind of what everybody thought they were doing with drugs, although in fact the drugs are only making them more remote, more selfish, more paranoid. If the true empathy were made manifest, then when somebody cut their knee, everybody would feel it. It wouldn't be complete loss of identity, but people would start to buoy each other up. They'd be able to sympathize with each other a lot more, and maybe cure each other's cancer.

"I've got a song where I say, 'We are all different versions of the same thing.' I'd love to believe that, but there are many people who are so hostile I can't even believe that they are the same species as me. I look at a fascist kid or something, and I think these creatures are not my species. I think there has got to be a physical change, and when this happens most of our art will become irrelevant. Things like Shakespeare's and Dostoevsky's writings won't mean anything because we won't be in that same kind of pain that humanity was in when those words were written."

Fear of the body and sexual terror, frequent themes in Hitchcock's work, seem at odds with his embrace of the Gaia theory, which suggests that the universe has its own natural intelligence and perfection. "I think that the more brutality I'm aware of, the more I appreciate what beauty is. Does that mean we need insane extremes to keep us upright? I don't really know. If I am disturbed by sex, or revolted by the body, maybe it's because I was shocked for such a long time by even being in a body. For the first thirty-five to forty years, it was quite a shock; you know, what am I doing in this incarnation? Maybe I have moved beyond that existentialist phase now, but we don't really know if there's anybody in our body or not. We don't know if we are supposed to exist or not. Our bodies may be valuable condos that we've queued up for millennia to inhabit, for which we've given some cosmic realtor so many karmic credits. So maybe we did ask to be born, in which case we should have some respect for the existence that we have. It's certainly worth it to value what you've got, even in the midst of bewailing what you have.

"I'm a very religious person, I just don't worship at any particular shrine. I think specific gods are a substitute for your parents. When you're little, you can hold up your hand and someone big will reach down and hold it. As you get bigger, there's nobody to reach up to anymore, and this has freaked people out over the generations. So they've invented Jehovah and Christ and Allah and Odin and Sol and Hecate and God knows how many of them, and they try and placate these gods, just like kids try to please their parents when they're mad at them.

"But the sacredness that's implicit in religion is very important. Although it's inevitable that most of the world's major religions are in decline except for fundamentalism, the sense of sacredness is really important. Life is sacred, life is magical, life is beyond our understanding. Life comes from something we don't know and is going somewhere we cannot get to yet. But humans, if anything can be said for us, have got prying minds, and we'll keep jumping up and down until we can see over the fence and find out what's there.

"I don't know what I'm really doing with my life as a musician. Music just points you somewhere and you have to follow it. It used to be just entertainment, and then this stuff came up in the sixties about singers being philosopher kings and shamans. They were supposed to be so much more than just singers. I grew up in those times, and although I knew that ultimately they were just sexy-looking guys in tight trousers who had a way with words, I felt that people like Dylan and Lennon and Jim Morrison still stumbled across the truth in some way.

"I never wanted to be a god, because I don't think humans can stand that. Humans are mortal, they exist in time and they crack. If you achieved godhood, it wouldn't be through becoming a pop star, because in the end you will fall, just as they've all fallen. You know, rock stars are all there on sufferance. They're there because they're making billions for the record company and the management and so they're allowed to have a few million for themselves. They're allowed to exist because they generate money for the business.

"The truth is I'm not sure if I'm a philosopher or a comedian, but I love music, and little bits of my philosophy must drip through into what I play. I should probably meditate and get the third eye going, but I think I'm evolving some understanding of the universe, I think I'm beginning to get an idea. I think you crash into things and by crashing into things, you realize where they are. Eventually you realize where everything is and you avoid falling out of the window every time you want to go to the bathroom."

PM DAWN

Rap's Alternative Spirituals

It was about 137 degrees Fahrenheit in New York City the day I interviewed PM Dawn, and it seemed like the man upstairs was trying to cook us alive. Maybe he was blowing off some steam. Maybe he was mad because PM hadn't been heard from much since their hit single a few years back called "I'd Die without You," from the sound track to Eddie Murphy's *Boomerang*. Maybe the man upstairs didn't like *Boomerang*. Anyway, it was hot that day.

PM Dawn was one of the bands parodied in the "spinal rap" movie called *Fear of a Black Hat*. In that satire of the rap world the two brothers from Jersey City were represented sitting on a grassy hill in rainbow-colored dashikis, singing dreamy, psychedelic hippie songs on the subject of making doodies. The movie mocked PM Dawn alongside rappers like Ice Cube, 2 Live Crew, Public Enemy, and N.W.A., which was funny but unfair. PM Dawn are funny next to Biggie Smalls, but so is Harry Nilsson.

In other words, don't judge PM Dawn as a rap act and maybe you'll enjoy them. Yes, they're a little hippie-dippy. Yes, they wear little round blue sunglasses. Yes, they sing about love and Christ consciousness, in multisyllabic descriptions of mystical visions (there are twenty-eight words in the titles of their first two albums alone). But might the fact that all this makes your average "real" rap-

per want to beat the stuffings out of PM Dawn mean there's something wrong with hip-hop, not the other way around? If hip-hop is going to continue to mature and expand as a music and culture, it's got to recognize that "reality," after all, isn't just other people's money, other people's girlfriends, and your own lightweight, German-made automatic pistol. Maybe that's what PM Dawn meant on their first big hit single, "Reality Used to Be a Friend of Mine." Maybe they were saying, Fuck hip-hop's version of reality. I can't be friends with a reality that only includes hardness. It's all yang and no yin. It's not realistic.

Hip-hop needs PM Dawn to complete itself. In Chinese martial arts they have a word for this: jou. It means soft, but soft like a snake. Soft like young bamboo. Soft like a shark. It means we need a few mushy-headed, peace-loving mystics who can actually sing in tune to balance out the armies of cold-eyed Brooklyn hard-rocks whose atonal rapping—beautiful and ominous as it is—cannot by itself describe reality.

Unfortunately, the rap universe hasn't realized this. And maybe that's why PM Dawn's third album, *Jesus Wept* (Gee Street/Island), has almost no rapping at all. Maybe there are other reasons. Maybe Prince Be/Reasons, the group's singer, who mysteriously added the word *Reasons* to the end of his name, knows why.

That terribly hot day, we met at a place called City Crab. Seated directly in front of a giant air conditioner vent, the three-hundred-pound-ish rapper snarfed up two appetizers at once as he thought about where rap was headed and whether he wanted to go there. "I didn't really want to rap anymore, because I thought people were overlooking me as an artist," says Prince Be/Reasons. "People assume that most hip-hop artists are substandard, musically. That's not necessarily the case. On the other hand, I don't ever wanna be portrayed as a hip-hop artist. I never diss it, but it's weird how I always get dissed by other hip-hop artists for not being *with* hip-hop. This time, I didn't want to associate myself with hip-hop, in terms of my vocals. On my new album, there's actually only one song out of fourteen that has a rap on it."

"I think I'd be a real threat to hip-hop if I said, 'Hip-hop can suck my dick,' but I love hip-hop. I was a hip-hop producer first. But as an artist you have to incorporate how you feel, and if you're not like someone else, or if you're not in the same vein, you just get fucked up by the whole rap scene."

PM Dawn's most recent album, *Jesus Wept*, dedicates one of its songs to "Christ consciousness," but PM Dawn are not born-again Christians. Although Be and his brother J.C. were raised in the church, today both are critical of organized religion, emphasizing the importance of individual inquisitiveness and the need to constantly call authority into question.

"I'm not gonna downplay organized religion," says Prince Be/Reasons, "because it makes a lot of sense for someone who doesn't know anything, but you have to start to ask questions eventually. Me, I'm just a stubborn bastard, and you can't just tell me to do something without giving me an explanation. If you're talking about worshiping God, I need an explanation for it. You can't just take someone's word when it comes to something as important as your own spirituality.

"So I pretty much like to make my own religion. I don't go to church, but I respect God. Christ consciousness seems to me like a logical thing, because it overtakes the masses rather than just one person. In Jesus, it overtook one person, but even Jesus said, 'All of these things I can do, you can do, too, even better.' But everybody sort of downplays that."

One reflection of PM Dawn's commitment to their spirituality is that on *Jesus Wept* they have forgone that one staple of all pop music in the twentieth century: the love song. Instead, they wrote love songs to a higher power, or, as they like to call them, alternative spirituals.

"I think nobody knows what spirituality is, and everybody interprets it their own way. Thing about it is, everybody thinks that their way is the shit and nobody else's opinion matters. You know, those holy wars: my spirituality is better than yours!

"I don't want to write love songs anymore. To sing a song you have to feel it. I can feel love, but it's not always between a man and a woman; there's many areas where love can exist. To me these songs have their own lives because they can mean different things to anyone at different times. Even though I write them, a lot of times I don't know what my songs are about until after they're finished. A song just sort of makes its own sense and I'm not gonna try to condition it to be a certain way. It sort of takes its own time to be its own person, just like when you have a child."

Before the songs on *Jesus Wept* were written, Prince Be underwent a period of intense silence for three weeks, during which he didn't speak a word. "I wanted to watch the world rather than interact with it," he says. "When you interact with other people, you have to take in what they say, and take in what they mean. I wanted to make sure I was who I was in terms of my own spirituality." When the bulk of the recording was finished, PM Dawn decided to take the album to a higher level. They walked around at a carnival with a tape recorder, Andy Warhol-style, and asked people why God loves them. (One young man, who responded, "God is my nigger, God is my *man!*" made it onto the album.) Then J.C. and Prince Be headed down to Atlanta with their cassette deck and recorded the sounds of silence at the grave of Martin Luther King Jr. "We got twenty-one seconds of silence," says Be, "because seven-seven-seven are positive numbers. Martin Luther King is an idol, and, to me, an example of Christ consciousness in its physical form. I wanted to give him that reverence."

For all of hip-hop's bravado, most rappers are reluctant to come out and talk about the complete truth of what it means to be human, especially when it comes to an honest examination of their own personal philosophy. In that sense, maybe PM Dawn is one of the bravest hip-hop acts around. The issue of how difficult it is to be yourself is raised most notably in the song "Downtown Venus." "You could be into you but you don't know what you're like," Prince Be sings, in a wash of buzzing harmonic guitars. "It's a song about self-awareness," says Be. "It kind of talks about your own divinity, in terms of how you achieve it and how you accept it. You don't really need anybody else, you don't need me to tell you that. It's just something that people naturally have and can manifest within themselves.

"A lot of people are afraid. They have stars and icons because they're afraid to tell themselves that they're worth a lot fucking more than they think they are. As much as people respect artists, they should feel that respect for themselves. I don't really separate myself from the people that surround me, and it should be that way with everybody. If they're not gonna understand their own divinity, I'm gonna understand it for them."

VERNON REID

A Psychology of Connecting the Dots

Between sips of pumpkin soup and long thoughtful glances of his puppy-dog eyes, Vernon Reid is talking, pausing, recollecting, and reflecting on his childhood, his upbringing in the Catholic Church, and his life in music. We're sitting in a cool little lunch box of a room on Ninth Avenue, just south of the Port Authority, and the people who populate this neighborhood—mental patients, bike messengers, prostitutes, meat packers, and oddball Hell's Kitchen businessmen—do not recognize Reid, founder of the Black Rock Coalition and the seminal band Living Colour. With his tousled chic, ungroomed dreadlocks, and baggy attire, he could be one of the local low-rent freaks, but as he settles in at a Formica table, he is recognized by one of the Swedish waitresses. He's not exactly model good-looking, but he's got a mischievous glimmer about him, a combination of arty intelligence and streetwise playfulness.

Born in London and raised in Brooklyn, Reid is generally numbered among the greats of rock guitar. But he hasn't an ounce of rock star in his personal presence—none of the damaged cool of Keith Richards, the crass slickness of Eddie Van Halen, or the burned-out professorial air of Eric Clapton. He's more like a Rasta version of Inspector Gadget. He has a gentle, easygoing demeanor, a comforting combination of clarity, patience, and exuber-

ance. In another life he might easily have been the host of some multicultural educational show on PBS. But the wave of psychedelic rock splashed over his life while he was a parochial-school student in the late sixties, washing away some of the shyness of the Catholic schoolboy who read books on dinosaurs while the others were learning to dance and play spin the bottle.

These days, any vestiges of Reid's nerdy demeanor have been worn smooth by his rock-star résumé. After founding Living Colour in 1985, he led the band on a steep climb to fame that included a Grammy-winning 1988 debut album entitled *Vivid* that sold two million copies and earned the band a slot opening for the Rolling Stones on their stadium tour the next year. Living Colour's follow-up album, *Times Up*, won the band their second Grammy Award for best rock performance, a unique feat for an all-black band. But Living Colour failed to connect with the "kids" during the first Lollapalooza tour—because alternative rock had become even more conformist than the mainstream rock it replaced, or because you couldn't slam dance to Living Colour's downtown art-damaged music. Either way, the band's third album, *Stain*, was a commercial disappointment, and the band broke up in 1995.

Reid, however, has remained active, collaborating with a wide range of musicians and working as a solo artist. The fact that he continues to make music that transcends racial pigeonholes is his most enduring victory. Beyond his music Reid is best known for the pioneering role he played in cofounding the Black Rock Coalition, an organization devoted to the struggle against institutional bias and the ghettoization of black music. He's also an accomplished writer and photographer, contributing essays to the *Village Voice* and *Vibe,* and occasionally showing his black-and-white photos in New York galleries.

At thirty-seven, Reid is both a rock and roll guitar fantasy come true *and* a consummate New Yorker: he's intellectual, fast talking, neurotic, interested in Taoism, knowledgeable about Buddhism, and fascinated with developmental childhood psychology. He is an improbable combination of Jimi Hendrix and Spaulding Grey.

Mistaken Identity, Reid's first solo album since Living Colour, combines his own distorted rock guitar with reggae, hip-hop, and fusion influences. Featuring jazz and klezmer clarinetist Don Byron, rapper Chubb Rock, and "found" orchestral elements performed by the London Philharmonic over forty years ago, *Mistaken Identity* reflects a quintessential New York outlook. As Reid told *Billboard* magazine, "The album is about that New York mentality, of being exposed to everything. Like when you're walking down the street here, and the music comes at you from different cars. There'll be Metallica coming from one and mixing with jeep beats from another. I've always thought, 'Man, I want to do something that sounds like that.' "

Mistaken Identity's title points to Reid's sense of himself as permanent outsider. Born in Britain to Caribbean immigrant parents, then moving to Brooklyn's great melting pot, he never felt he belonged fully to the culture of America, England, or the Caribbean. "My parents are from the West Indies, and I guess it could be said that I am too, but my 'Caribbean-ness' is a very abstract thing, because I never visited the islands until much later in my life.

"The thing about the British islands is that a lot of them are Catholic. My parents came from Montserrat, which is a British island, so I was raised Catholic. When people think of black churches, they think of Baptists, and shouting and singing, that kind of expression, but when you're raised Catholic it's a completely different thing."

Although he expresses great reverence for his parents, Reid's attitude toward the religion he inherited from them is ambivalent. "When I started going to church it was the early sixties, the mass was still in Latin, so all the rituals and ceremonies were very serious, and I didn't know what they meant. My parents were very observant. They worked a lot, my father at the post office for many years, and my mother for various union organizations. It was a little strange growing up. I felt alone a lot. I was close with my parents, but I felt a kind of existential loneliness. I guess I related to Jesus as a kind of loner character. Nobody understood him and they crucified him in the end.

"Early on, I was attracted to otherworldly stuff—science fiction, comic books, horror movies. The idea of the unknown looms really large for me. I remember being afraid yet fascinated at an early age. I was absolutely terrified of a show like *The Twilight Zone*, but I had to watch it every week. So I'm not really frightened of the unknown, because I'm attracted to it."

The strictness and blind faith associated with Reid's Catholic-school upbringing were difficult for him to swallow. A literal interpretation of the Bible just didn't fit with the humanistic, scientifically oriented personality Reid displayed from an early age, and the heavy-handed discipline left an indelible mark on him.

"At that time, Catholic school was not 'feel-good,' it was not 'touchy-feely.' Corporal punishment was the order of the day. It was unfair, and humiliating and brutalizing, and many of my classmates were victimized by it. The rule of adults was based on the idea that 'We can do this because we're bigger than you.' I saw kids get struck, knocked off their feet, slapped into hysterics, for the smallest offenses, and I reflect upon it now with more than a little anger."

Reid's perspective on the church today sounds decidedly Freudian, as he emphasizes the unconscious needs and desires of the saints and acolytes who organized the church. "In many ways, Christians are only beginning to study the psychology of early figures like Saint Augustine and the degree to which their system is an expression of certain psychological traumas of ancient history. Like, the idea of God being a parent who demands your love, but with the threat of ultimate violence at the end of it. Or the idea of Lucifer, the best and brightest in heaven, essentially kicked out of the house.

"The thing that I would say about my parents is that they're really kindly people in terms of the way they implemented religion in their lives. It wasn't beaten over my head. I had a lot of interesting talks with my father, because he was a cat who believed in science and believed in natural law, so I never got the idea that the world was created in seven days. He was not at all fundamentalist. I was just with my parents last night, and I love them, they are great, fantastic people. It's just that all of us are part of this chain of unresolved stuff, and we pass it on. The trauma comes from parent to child and so on through the generations."

Speaking of the times when his parents' hands were raised against him, Reid says: "I can't turn around and say it was a horror story—it wasn't. But when it happened, it was humiliating. And it's like, what did I do wrong? Nothing was being explained. It's like a shortcut. When I was a kid I said to myself, I never want anyone to feel this kind of humiliation, and I think about it constantly now, before I even get to the point of being a parent myself."

Because of his parents' Caribbean heritage, Reid grew up in a household with a rich musical mix of early ska and calypso records imported from the islands, British invasion bands, and jazz. Despite her unquestioning devotion to the church, his mother owned every James Brown single released in the 1960s, many of which, like "Sex Machine," were decidedly unchurchy.

"I was sort of known for my weirdness, you know, like my interest in dinosaurs and alternate universes, but because I loved music so much, somehow or other I learned to dance when I was in high school, and I learned to be more social. Although Sly Stone, the Beatles, and Hendrix were all inspirations, it was Carlos Santana who loomed largest. I had heard 'Oye Como Va,' and I was really struck by his sound. I got my first guitar when I was fifteen. Then I met up with some guys who were in a jazz workshop at Brooklyn Tech, with a teacher named Gene Ghee who played records—rock and roll and jazz—and talked about theory. The first time I heard Coltrane was around 1972, when Mr. Ghee played 'My Favorite Things.' He was a great teacher and a big influence."

At this point in his adolescence, Reid was on his way to becoming an agnostic. "I'd still go to church at Christmas and Easter, but it seemed to me that underlying all of it was a threat. The Christian is compelled to love God with all his heart, he's *compelled* to do it. You're supposed to do it of your own free will, but you *have* to do it. There is no choice involved, because to choose another way is to be in error, as the church often says, and it is to risk the wrath.

"God's personality always confused me because on one hand, God is merciful, kind, and loving, but on the other he's wrathful and vengeful. He's like this implacable parent whose motives you're not supposed to know, and the relationship that people have with God in organized religion in many ways mirrors the relationships that children are forced to have with parents. You don't know what they're thinking, they're not communicating with you, but you have to do the things you're ordered to, and you're supposed to be grateful for it.

"To me, science was at least one thing that made sense. The other thing, faith, didn't make sense. A lot of the evangelicals even say that you have to lose your mind, you have to surrender your intellectual process, to things that are nonsensical. It's nonsensical that someone could live inside a whale. It's allegory. It's a mythology. It's a myth that people were simpler and more honest at some time in the past. People had complicated motivations, always. People were always capable of the most egregious cruelties and the most amazing bravery, courage, and compassion. It's always been that way."

Raymond Jones, a piano player that Reid met in high school, played a pivotal role in helping him decide to become a professional musician. "Raymond asked me, 'What do you wanna do when you get out of here?' Because Raymond knew. He said, 'I am a piano player, that's what I'm gonna do: I'm gonna play piano.' There was no doubt in his mind, and he was so good at it—he was a really remarkable jazz piano player for his age. It affected me and I started thinking seriously about becoming a musician."

After graduating from high school, Reid attended a community college, and his musical tastes began expanding into the realm of free jazz. "By that time I was really into Ornette Coleman, but I still liked Sly Stone and Parliament/Funkadelic and James Brown. For me music has always been additive, never subtractive: if I fall in love with something, I always love it. So for me, the Beatles are still in the house."

Reid started playing with a rhythm and blues producer named Kashif; it was his one attempt to fit into the preconceived role of the black musician in the pop music marketplace, and its failure would spur his interest in creating the Black Rock Coalition. "I kinda tried to fit in. I felt like, OK, I'll do this middle-of-the-road rhythm and blues thing. But it didn't work out and so I said, Well, I might as well do whatever the hell I want, because fitting in just isn't the thing for me."

Soon after leaving Kashif, Reid found himself playing guitar in jazz drummer Ronald Shannon Jackson's band, Decoding Society. "I saw Shannon Jackson playing with James 'Blood' Ulmer at the Public Theater and I was astounded at his energy and power. I thought, Wow, I really want to play with this guy. I met Shannon after the show and said, 'You were really great,' and I told him that I was a friend of his bass player, Melvin Gibbs. Then I got a call one day from Melvin, and he said. 'Shannon wants to hear you play, he wants to check you out,' So I came by and started playing and he just said, 'OK, rehearsal's next week.' "

It was through Ronald Shannon Jackson that Reid had his first close encounter with Eastern philosophy and meditation, although some of his musical heroes had already interested him in Buddhism and Hinduism, if only by association.

"I knew that Carlos Santana and John McLaughlin were followers of Sri Chinmoy, and my friend the guitarist Arthur Rhames was a Hare Krishna. I started listening to Indian music, and that was a pathway to an exposure to alternative ways of thinking about spirituality. I heard some of Alan Watts's lectures on the radio and I was taken with the musical sound of his voice. There was a kind of erudition and playfulness with him, as well as with Aldous Huxley.

"Ronald Shannon Jackson was a Buddhist, a follower of the Nichiren school, and playing with him I was exposed to Buddhist thought. Shannon kinda left me alone, which was cool, because he was very strong in his practice, and within the Nichiren tradition of Buddhist practice there's a degree of proselytizing. I kind of kept my distance from it, although I did chant once with him and a couple of the other members of the band who had become Buddhists. Saying these phrases reminded me of a Latin mass. I didn't think it was meaningless, I just felt it was very arcane. To Shannon's credit, he didn't force it on me and I didn't continue to chant."

While Reid had long felt that there was more to spiritual life than the Catholic masses of his childhood, until then he had never had any formal instruction in meditation. "I would just sit quietly; that's what I thought meditation was. Sometimes it would help to quiet me down, because I have a monkey mind, as they call it in Buddhist practice, a chattering mind. It kind of goes here and there, and there are aspects of that I actually like, such as the ability to free-associate, to come up with ideas and associations that I might not normally make. Some of these connections are a little bit mysterious, because it's in the body, feeling a certain rhythm or melody, hearing things, paying attention to inner voices. Things that you know, things that you feel innately."

The meditative practice of paying precise attention to your state of mind can have a dramatic effect on the creative process. Playing what you feel—as opposed to what you "know" or are familiar playing—requires a kind of openness similar to the experience of meditation. "It is really interesting to correlate what I hear in the moment when I'm onstage and what I hear when there is no out-side force to affect me. I think the key thing is to open myself as much as I can. The goal is to have no expecta-tions or desires about what I want to feel or what I want people in the audience to feel, and to go wherever it's going.

"My practice at the time was just accepting where people were at. I hated this judgmental thing that religions put on people. But I was going out with a girl who had accepted the idea of Christ in her life, and she said to me, 'Vernon, you've got to give your soul an address.' That stayed with me, and I explored a little further, reading Lao Tzu and Zen books, thinking about the unity of all things and how 'object' and 'subject' are just constructed ideas."

It was during this time of spiritual exploring that Reid emerged from Ronald Shannon Jackson's band and formed the nucleus of what would become the Black Rock Coalition, and Living Colour. "When I left Shannon Jackson, I got together with my friends to play for fun. The band went through various changes and became Living Colour. The whole Black Rock Coalition thing was just a gathering of friends to find out whether other people shared my conceptions about the music industry."

It is interesting that Reid was developing the Black Rock Coalition at the same time that he was digesting Buddhism and Taoism, because activism and spirituality have not always been easy to reconcile. In some people's eyes, the church has historically been an instrument of black passivity, and on the surface at least, Buddhism, with its emphasis on acceptance, appears even more difficult to reconcile with the activist stance of black nationalism and pride. "With regard to the idea of a specifically 'black' approach to spiritual practice, the fact is that none of us asked to be born, and when we are born, we are at the behest of people who are deeply damaged and conflicted. Someone asked me about how it was important for me to be black, and I said, 'The reason that I'm black is that you're white.' In reality, this idea of race completely breaks down; if you go to a place that's racially homogeneous, then what is the conflict about? You have to put it into context: black is defined against white, so we're talking about a game of identities."

Still, the Black Rock Coalition wasn't called the Human Musician's Coalition. It was called the Black Rock Coalition for good reason: "We were working with the way people think. The music industry is not supporting or recognizing a wide range of music by black people and the Black Rock Coalition was about confronting that. You wouldn't need a White Rock Coalition because rock is so dominated by white people. The idea of struggle was very much a part of the Black Rock Coalition. Although I felt there was a deeper reality, the fact that racism, slavery, grandfathering, and redlining have given a certain segment of the population a historical advantage needs to be factored into the equation."

Unlike many activists, Reid knows that the struggle is ultimately about something deeper than the financial and social inequalities associated with racism. He knows that material wealth alone will not make black people happy, any more than it's made whites happy. "Material things have not lessened the deeper suffering of white people. Suffering is relative; you can suffer if you're a millionaire and feel guilty about it because you're not really supposed to suffer. Look at Kurt Cobain: there's someone who on some level must have felt that he had no right to suffer. You think, 'I have no right to feel the way I'm feeling,' so you close off your feelings."

Today, Reid remains unaffiliated with any particular religion or school of thought, and his childhood interest in the natural sciences has not been dimmed by the years spent in search of some higher truth. "Even the basic laws of physics seem like spiritual laws to me; like, every action has an equal and opposite reaction. Making correlations between Western psychotherapy and Eastern Buddhism is of great interest to me, because while Western psychology can give a very close analysis of why someone's suffering, Buddhist practice can actually provide a way to end suffering.

"I'm not arrogant enough to assume that I can get to where I'm going completely by myself, but the funny thing about enlightenment is that it's like you're searching for something—say your hat—and you're tearing the house apart and suddenly you look in a mirror and you see it sitting on top of your head.

"Music is where I've experienced that. I'm in a flow, I'm in the zone, there's a definite shift in my consciousness, without desire, without my ego, without me thinking, oh wow, I'm playing great. Just experiencing it as a flowing, living moment. Once you've experienced it, you always know that's a place to go to.

"The thing is, you can't make it happen. It's not about how much you practice, it's not about whether your record's on the charts. It exists independently of those things, and it makes you aware that there are processes that are going on in playing music that are much deeper. The most difficult thing is to let go after you've felt it. You have to let go of the experience. Then gradually, by watching your mind work, by really being in the living moment, the experience becomes more common. Any musician can be the greatest musician in the world on a particular night. The thing about the masters is that they do it consistently. The thing about Coltrane is that he went there lots of times.

"So if it's there within you, how do you coax it out? I think you just have to prepare yourself and be open for this gift and accept the fact that it's not always going to be there. Just remain open. Keep preparing yourself for it to happen. And enjoy the moments that are not these super-enlightened moments. Enjoy the rhythm, just the groove of the thing, just the song itself."

Photo Credits

Perry Farrell: Photo by C. B. Smith. Philip Glass: Photo by Carol Rosegg, courtesy of Point Music. Joan Osborne: Photo by Wayne Isaac, courtesy of Mercury Records. Ziggy Marley: Photo by Marc Baptiste, courtesy of Electra Entertainment. Mick Jagger: Photo by Max Vadukul. Meredith Monk: Photo by Jesse Frohman. Moby: Photo by Anna Gabriel. Iggy Pop: Photo by Kate Lacey. Michael Franti: Photo by Kwaku Alston, courtesy of Capitol Records. Nusrat Fateh Ali Khan: Photo by Jack Vartoogian. Allen Ginsberg: Photo by Robert Frank, courtesy of Mercury Records. Jeff Buckley: Photo by Bruce Weber. Dead Can Dance: Photo of Lisa Gerrard by Rob Grierson, courtesy of 4 AD; Photo of Brendan Perry by Linda Elvira Piedra, courtesy of 4 AD. Al Green: Photo by Carol Friedman, courtesy of MCA. Billy Bragg: Photo by Steve Double, courtesy of Elektra Entertainment. Leonard Cohen: Photographer unknown, courtesy of Stranger Management. The Reverend Run: Photo by Anna Gabriel. Robyn Hitchcock: Photo by Kate Lacey. PM Dawn: Photo by Anna Gabriel. Vernon Reid: Photo by Anna Gabriel.

About the Author

Dimitri Ehrlich is a musician and music journalist who has written about music for the *New York Times, New York* magazine, *Vibe, Entertainment Weekly, Mademoiselle, Rolling Stone,* and *Spin.* He was a music editor at *Interview* magazine for five years and is now music editor at MTV.

Dimitri Ehrlich is also a singer and songwriter. His band, "Dimitri and the Supreme 5000," has received national critical acclaim for their debut album *Everything is Naked* (Fierce Records u.s.a.). To hear a sampling of their music, visit http://www.dimitrimusic.com